Woody Allen

WOODY ALLEN

A Life in Film

RICHARD SCHICKEL

Ivan R. Dee

CHICAGO

The paperback edition of this book carries the ISBN 1-56663-602-7.

Library of Congress Cataloging-in-Publication Data:
Schickel, Richard.
    Woody Allen : a life in film / Richard Schickel.
        p. cm.
    Includes index.
        ISBN 1-56663-528-4 (alk. paper)
        1. Allen, Woody—Interviews. 2. Motion picture producers and directors—United States—Interviews. I. Title.
        PN1998.3.A45A5 2003
        791.43'092—dc21   2003055112

For

Doug Freeman

Chris Vild

Peter Ballenger

from their bedazzled father-in-law

A Note on the Text

TYPICALLY, a director gets to use no more than 20 percent—if that—of the interviews he conducts for a documentary film. In the case of my very lengthy talk with Woody Allen—it consumed about four hours and covered, at least briefly, every aspect of his career as a filmmaker—I felt that virtually the whole thing was interesting and worth preserving. Hence publication of the text that follows, on which I have done only minor editing.

As an interviewer my style tends to be more conversational than bluntly interrogative. So I've cut some of my questions in order to bring them more quickly to the point. As for Woody, he is never wholly comfortable talking about his own work, so there was more than the usual number of stammered beginnings in his responses. These I simply cut. He also had a tendency to respond to a question fairly briefly, think it over, then add to that response—but, in the process, repeat his initial statement. In a few cases I conflated these statements. Finally, about a year later, I conducted another interview with Woody about Charles Chaplin, about whom I was doing another documentary. I liked what he said about Chaplin so much that I inserted a few paragraphs from that conversation at the appropriate places in this text. But nothing significant has been cut from this interview. As far as I know, Woody has still not seen the film I made about him—he says that when he's old and out of it he may look at it, but cautions that by that time he'd probably be too dim to recognize himself—and he has, of course, not seen this manuscript either. Therefore I take full responsibility for its sins of omission and commission.

R. S.

Los Angeles
June 2003

Woody Allen

Introduction
Woody in the Afternoon

AS OF THIS MOMENT (February 2003) Woody Allen has written and directed thirty-two feature films (and one-third of an anthology piece) in the thirty-four years since he decided, in the late sixties, that he would not make a movie unless he was its sole and unquestioned author. This resolve has occasionally weakened. He has appeared in some movies he neither wrote nor directed, and he has allowed others to direct adaptations of his plays, *Don't Drink the Water* and *Play It Again, Sam*. Still, his record is astonishing—essentially one film a year since *Take the Money and Run* in 1969—and quite unmatched by any contemporary American filmmaker.

You would have to go back to the thirties and forties, when the studios were organized along factory lines, to find contract directors whose filmographies match the length of Woody's. But these craftsmen didn't usually write their pictures. Or act in them, as Woody has in the majority of his films. Nor did the studios usually grant their directors a large say in the casting, editing, scoring, promoting, or advertising of their pictures (Alfred Hitchcock would be a notable exception), all of which Woody intensely attends. Nor did any of these directors have Woody's busy sidelines as a playwright and writer of humorous pieces.

You have to look elsewhere to find careers like Woody's. In Europe, Ingmar Bergman has created a body of work comparable in independence and fecundity (though of course Woody would resist any other comparison between his work and Bergman's). Some people have evoked Charles Chaplin's career as in some ways analogous to Woody's. As performers, both, for the most part, played a single, highly defined character. As filmmakers, both functioned with utter independence—Chaplin because he self-financed all but one of his features, Woody because he will not accept backing from anyone threatening to interfere with his vision. Some observers have even compared their personal lives, since both men, late in life, scandalized press and public by taking up relationships with much younger women—though not much is made of the fact that both belatedly achieved contentment in those relationships.

But even this comparison breaks down. Chaplin, once he began making feature-length films, famously slowed his production pace. Between 1924 and 1967 he made only ten movies, less than one-third the number Woody created in a similar time frame and, masterpieces (*A Woman of Paris, The Circus, City Lights*) aside, not necessarily a better body of work overall than Woody's—more aspiring perhaps, but not better.

The difference is largely one of anticipation. The world—perhaps incorrectly—expects more of any artistic creation that has obviously been toiled over for years than it does of one that appears to be tossed off. Moreover, Chaplin's later works took up big, obvious social themes—the alienation of labor, fascism, capitalist iniquities—whereas Woody's movies rarely touch on such matters.

Woody's work suffers in this kind of comparison. It has come to be taken for granted by his small American audience, almost as if the annual release of a Woody Allen film is akin to an unimportant national holiday—noted in passing but not celebrated, except by a minority who have made a long-standing, almost habitual, commitment to it; in a way, it's like the Italians with Columbus Day or the Irish with St. Patrick's Day. Even Woody's loyalists often strike a somewhat querulous note when they talk about his most recent movies.

In a way this is understandable. With some notable exceptions, Woody continues to set his movies in the milieu he began exploring with the widely beloved *Annie Hall*—urban, middlebrow, prosperous (and now aging)—and it feels to them as if this is still the same-old, same-old. About this the audience is sometimes wrong. Yes, these films are still often about romantic misalliances, in which the principals are discovered in a state of restlessness or open rebellion with their relationships, embark on new ones, and end up not much better off. But even when Woody maintains the conventions of what we might call the anti-romantic comedy, as he more or less single-handedly developed them many years ago, he has, within that form, greatly expanded his subtexts and refined his style.

Indeed, it might be said that he can match Chaplin—or anyone else one might name—in his attraction to great (and insoluble) existential issues we as individuals inevitably encounter. In this essay I particularly want to stress the fact that many of Woody's most memorable films have, largely unnoticed but uniquely, brought over from literature to the movies the manner (and substance) of "magic realism," that "phenomenon characterized by the incorporation of fantastic and mythical elements matter-of-factly into otherwise realistic fiction," as one literary dictionary defines it.

It interests me that this point has been so little remarked in the vast critical literature that has accreted around Woody's work in the last quarter-century. So much of it has been devoted to calculating this film or that's relative standing on the laffometer. Or to wishing Woody would do something more in the vein of *Bananas*.

All these—and more—are topics that preoccupied Woody when I interviewed him for several hours in the fall of 2001, excerpts of which formed the basis of the ninety-minute television program I made about him and his films for Turner Classic Movies, and which is here reprinted in slightly edited form. In introducing that interview I want to expand on it critically and attempt something that, to my knowledge, has not previously been tried: an analysis of Woody's movies—more or less in order—in terms of their developing thematic interconnections.

I think, in all immodesty, that I am well situated for this task. In order to conduct my interview I watched all of

Woody's movies in a very short span of time—less than a month. It's fairly rare for a critic to so immerse himself in a single artist's work. Mostly one sees a director's work as it appears and one is forced to depend on always fallible memory to notice the new piece's congruities and incongruities with what preceded it. Moreover, one usually does not have a chance to talk with the artist in question immediately after such an immersion. (Indeed, Woody once or twice murmured, in the course of our talk, that I had the advantage of him, because he had not recently seen any of his older films while I had.) Finally, in the six-month course of putting our program together, I was repeatedly exposed to significant pieces of his work on a daily basis. In short, I claim a certain recent authority on Woody's work that is not, at the moment, matched by anyone else.

Beyond that, I have a longer-term sympathy with it. The record of my respect for it is spread over three decades of movie reviewing and several longer profiles I have written about Woody. Part of this regard is generational. We are roughly the same age; we read the same books, saw the same movies, dreamed similarly of big-city lives (he was born in Brooklyn, I was born in Milwaukee, but we were both, emotionally speaking, equidistant from the Manhattan spires to which we jointly aspired).

This says nothing about the things we quite independently learned to distrust—organized religion, conventional (or revolutionary) politics, corporate America, faddish self-improvement, whether it involves diets, popularized mysticism, or, for that matter, aromatherapy. We are, I think, most basically existentialists, haunted by death, the silence of the universe, the absence of God, dependent on work to distract us from the surrounding nothingness, yet glumly convinced that it too is just a way to pass the time between cradle and grave.

I do not have an intimate relationship with Woody Allen. We met casually a long time ago, making our youthful, hopeful rounds in New York. We began to acknowledge one another a little more formally as our careers developed, and we've shared a few pleasant social and professional occasions over the years. But I believe my bias in favor of his work would exist even if I had never met him. It simply speaks to me—and *for* me sometimes—in a quite uncomplicated way. And I am bound to say that if you, the reader, do not share that bias, you are reading the wrong book.

2

Woody's watershed movie—the film in which he clearly annunciated the ideas and the manner that would form what I think of as the most significant line of his work, and began the process of loosening such hold as he had on the mainstream audience—was *Stardust Memories,* released in 1980. I have to say that at the time it troubled me as much as it troubled the rest of his audience. I have returned to it more often than to any of his other films, trying to gain both a critical and an emotional purchase on it.

In the film he played Sandy Bates, a character who seemed to be suspiciously like himself—or if not like himself, then like the self he imagined he might become or his admirers feared he might already be. His Sandy is a comic filmmaker who, like Woody at that time, has started making somewhat more serious movies. He attends a retrospective weekend devoted to screenings and discussions of his work and is assaulted on every hand by fans who keep telling him how much they love his movies, "especially the early funny ones." In his interview with me, Woody insists that he meant no disrespect to his audience or to his own early funny ones—*Bananas* or *Love and Death* or *Sleeper*. He was just trying to be—well—funny, using a line he had surely heard others use in reference to his own work. In fact he does not disown his early work; it was, he says, "pleasurable" for him to make. And profitable too. Besides, as he observes, *Stardust Memories* was essentially a long dream sequence, a projection of his anxieties, perhaps, but not an accurate statement about his own well-controlled and comfortably managed reality.

Stardust Memories remains one of the few of his own movies that Woody speaks kindly of—perhaps because it represents a major step forward in terms of technique, possibly because it is quite bitterly truthful about the ways fame can disrupt and distort a life even when you are doing your best not to let it do so. But it was, as he well knows, his first film to be greeted with fairly general critical dubiety and audience discomfort.

In talking with him, I suggested that perhaps celebrity is the one subject that is forbidden to celebrities. Whatever they may have to say on the topic is almost bound to seem self-serving—if not self-pitying. Woody flatly rejected that idea. But I cling to it, if only because open discussion of the emotional transactions that take place between the famous and the not famous—mysterious and sometimes fractious—breaks the silence on which that relationship depends. We all know that love dies the minute one or both parties begin to analyze it.

If we apply that idea to *Stardust Memories* we see that even though Sandy's film weekend is a dream, it is clearly informed by Woody's acute sense of the implied tensions between a famous person and his fans. On the one hand, they adore him precisely because he has captured and reflected back to them certain aspects of their experience that they may have vaguely felt but could never themselves express. This seems to them uncanny, almost a miracle.

On the other hand, their resentment is also profound. Dream or not, Woody presents almost everyone Sandy encounters in *Stardust Memories* as a grotesque—they jabber nonsense at him, they require objects he has touched or worn for celebrity auctions, they invade his bedroom looking for a celebrity fuck. A high school friend who has failed in life appears out of the shadows to test Sandy's compassion. His family grasps at him, trying to drag him back down into their miseries. Accountants and lawyers bring him bad news about tax audits. Studio executives demand he recut his new picture. The politically and socially aware criticize his lack of concern for the plight of the hungry, the ailing, the Jews. This is the darkest imaginable frenzy of renown.

And it is made all the more confusing for the audience because Woody appears to be appearing as himself. There is no makeup or accent for him to hide behind. He looks exactly as he does in all his films and as he does in life—a slightly built, vulnerably intelligent man wearing glasses and an air of befuddlement (if not downright panic) over the way his natural reserve has been penetrated, but still gamely spritzing wisecracks to cover his confusion, recover his balance.

That's the way the audience first saw him, first took him to heart, and they don't like to see him in a different light. They didn't realize that the Woody they first met doing stand-up routines in the clubs and on television was an act—an invented persona—even though he appeared under his own name. They didn't understand that Alvy Singer in *Annie Hall* or the *shleps* that preceded him were acts. They didn't know that Sandy Bates was an act. In some part of their souls they just don't understand that Woody Allen—despite the narrowness of range that he talks about in this interview—is, among other things, an actor, a man playing roles.

So when they confronted him as Sandy, they thought something had perhaps gone wrong with him. Perhaps he had grown too big for his britches, or anyway too big for their gratitude. Only three years earlier they had adored him and

Diane Keaton in *Annie Hall.* It had been—by Woody's modest standards—a commercial success, and it had won multiple Academy Awards. They had forgiven his descent into seriousness in *Interiors,* welcomed him back to good humor in the darkly romantic *Manhattan.* But now this . . . this transgression.

I don't claim that the alienation between Woody and the mainstream American movie audience definitively took place with *Stardust Memories.* After all, his greatest commercial success, *Hannah and Her Sisters,* occurred six years later. (I remember talking to Woody at the time and hearing him exclaim, wonderingly, "It's performing just like a regular picture," meaning that it was grossing not like a Woody Allen movie, but like a normally successful romantic comedy that anyone might have made.)

But I do think a breach was opened with *Stardust Memories.* And I do think that Woody widened it during the 1980s. Around that time I wrote somewhere that his audience had deserted him, and he corrected me in the excellent profile John Lahr wrote about him in *The New Yorker,* not long after his troubles with Mia Farrow made him into a figure of tabloid scandal. "I left my audience is what really happened; they didn't leave me."

I think, on reconsideration, that that's the truth. For as he also told Lahr: "I was gonna do films that had a harder edge, like *Husbands and Wives.* If I wanted to make a film like *Shadows and Fog,* I was not in any way going to live out my end of the contract with the audience. I was gonna break the contract. I hoped that they would come with me, but they didn't. . . . They were as nice as could be. If I had kept making *Manhattan* or *Annie Hall*—the same kind of pictures—they were fully prepared to meet me halfway."

Instead he made a group of films in the eighties and early nineties that constitute, in my opinion, one of the great runs of movies ever made by any director in a relatively short span of time. They include *Zelig, The Purple Rose of Cairo, Radio Days, Crimes and Misdemeanors,* and *Shadows and Fog.* Interspersed among them are the only marginally less gratifying *Broadway Danny Rose, Another Woman, Alice, Husbands and Wives, Deconstructing Harry,* and, of course, *Hannah.* This eleven years concludes with 1994's *Bullets over Broadway,* which I believe to be the most formally perfect of all his films.

If there has since been a falling off in the imaginative intensity of his work—and I think there has—it is not, to me, a matter of huge consequence. Most of his later films are enjoyable, with occasional flashes of brilliance—the Greek chorus in *Mighty Aphrodite,* or the hilarious representation of the actor's nightmare, the quite literal blurring of Robin Williams's image (both on screen and in life) in *Deconstructing Harry. Celebrity,* I thought, was much better than most of the reviewers did. And *Hollywood Ending,* the picture that provided the occasion for my television program, seemed to me to operate very smoothly out of a terrific comic premise—a difficult, essentially unemployable movie director, played by

Woody, is afflicted by psychosomatic blindness but must hide his condition and make his movie anyway—which I thought Woody quite happily sustained.

The American critics and audience disagreed with me, though the film went on to do profitable business in Europe, as most of his films do. (Woody has mentioned to me that several of his recent releases have done more business in Paris alone than they have in the entire United States; nowadays he obtains most of his financing abroad.)

But no matter. It seems to me that at sixty-seven Woody is entitled to relax some of the creative pressure he has habitually imposed on himself, to wind his movies less tightly, as in fact he did with *Curse of the Jade Scorpion* and *Small-time Crooks*—minor comic ideas he says he pulled from a drawer, but which may also have been unacknowledged (and unsuccessful) attempts to recapture some of the fine, careless rapture of his earlier relation with his audience.

Movies are a chancy business. It is entirely possible that Woody, before he is finished, will have another domestic hit. But I don't think it is highly likely. And I don't believe he thinks so either. The regard in which he is held in Europe sustains him comfortably economically and (perhaps) psychologically. Certainly those matters that exercised the American public—the vicious conflict with Mia Farrow, the lawsuit against his sometime friend and business partner, Jean Doumanian, which was quite difficult for newspaper readers to understand—seem to his overseas audience (as they do to me) quite irrelevant to the evaluation of his work, though not, alas, to the dubious regard in which many Americans now hold him as an individual.

3

I'll return—reluctantly—to these matters later. For the moment I want to concentrate on that run of extraordinary movies I just named. And I want to begin by saying that I agree with the Europeans: Woody's estrangement from the mass American audience (if we dare employ such a term in near proximity to his name) predates his tribulations with Farrow and Doumanian and is, in any event, a more interesting question to explore. It has primarily to do, I think, with his embrace of magic realism, specifically his belief that salvation is available to humankind only through the intervention of mysterious, inexplicable forces in our everyday lives.

His definitions of what form such transformative interventions might take are very loose—he's explored any number of variations on this theme, and, of course, he avoids the topic entirely in many of his films. Yet it is quite clear, from both his films and his conversation, that he continues to think—as he has from the late seventies onward—that pure rationalism is entirely inadequate to our needs.

The easy answer to his dilemma, embraced by billions the world over in some form or another, is conventional religious belief—in a God, in the immortality of the soul. Such belief is, to me, magic realism writ dangerously large. And Woody flatly rejects it. He does not even believe, as so many secular artists do, that they can achieve immortality through posterity's undying regard for their work. That idea, he says, is "the artist's Catholicism," which is to say, a nice consoling illusion but, practically speaking, a long shot.

This leaves him with luck. And with magic realism. In the former he is "a big believer." Or as he has also, more famously, said, "80 percent of life is just showing up." By this Woody means that if you put yourself in the way of opportunity— make yourself available to, say, a woman who is attractive to you, or some task you think you might be qualified for— something good may come of the fact that you are there and that someone else, perhaps equally qualified, is not. The corollary of that idea, of course, has to do with *not* showing up— not finishing your play or novel, not going to the audition, being so shy or insecure that you dare not risk failure.

He recognizes that this is not, for many of us, an entirely attractive philosophy. We believe in volition, believe that we are the masters of our fates, the captains of our souls. In a country as devoted as ours is to effortful self-improvement, to making ourselves fit and ready to seize destiny by the forelock, the idea that we are blown this way and that, toward success and failure, by the winds of chance, is a highly subversive one. It sounds, you know, *foreign.* And it also implies that we are wasting an awful lot of time and money on psychiatry or, for that matter, working out at the gym.

If, however, the artistic universe you are positing is pretty much the one I've just described, then magic realism becomes an appropriate strategy for capturing at least a measure of its essence. It is also a description that, to my knowledge, Woody has never publicly applied to his work and I have not encountered in any of the critical writing I have read about it—including my own.

But let's think a little more about magic realism as Woody has presented it. It begins, I think, in *Annie Hall* (written with Marshall Brickman), with the first serious conversation between Alvy and Annie, where they are trying to impress each other with their moral and intellectual seriousness while subtitles reveal their truer, raunchier thoughts. Later in the film, when their relationship has settled—as so many do in Woody Allen films—into unromantic routine, we see a ghostly Annie arise from their bed while they are making love, and start looking for her drawing pad—something more interesting to do while her other self and Alvy grimly pursue their orgasm.

These are both funny (and original) gags, and because they appear in a film by a famous funnyman that is how—simply—they were accepted by the audience. But they mark the beginning of a trend that would dominate Woody's filmmaking in the years to come.

He first made *Interiors,* which had perhaps the most realistic air of any of his films and which was, at the time, roundly rejected critically. This study of an almost completely dysfunctional upper-middle-class New York family seems to me much better now than it did when it first appeared. It is, in fact, a comedy in the Chekovian sense of the word—that is to say, a comedy with the jokes left out. Yet it is very touching and ironic about three variously tormented (by mortality, by unrealized ambition, by airheadedness) sisters coming to grips with their damaged and compulsive mother, the while rejecting the vulgar yet life-affirming stepmother whom their emotionally clueless father introduces to the family. It is an elegant movie, subtly lit and shot (by Gordon Willis), extremely fluid and self-effacing in directorial technique. Stylistically it represents a huge step forward for Woody.

That's a point worth bearing in mind as we traverse this career. Whatever you think about the content of his films, his craft has kept growing in sophistication. He proved he could do the kind of burnished realism this and his other urban anti-romances demanded, but he could also do the jumpier kind of reality demanded by, say, *Husbands and Wives* or *Deconstructing Harry,* or the *faux* documentary manner of *Zelig,* or the expressionism of *Shadows and Fog.* He has, virtually unremarked, become a truly masterful director.

His next film, *Manhattan* (also co-written with Brickman), was a success, critically and with the public, possibly because it reminded people somewhat of *Annie Hall* in that it was a wittily told story of a troubled romance. Again the movie, shot in black and white, had an extremely elegant quality (it was, among other things, Woody's handsomest pictorial tribute to his beloved New York). Like *Annie Hall* and *Interiors,* it developed another theme that would preoccupy Woody in varying degrees for the rest of his career. This was the way the urban chattering classes, full of brittle opinions about art and music and literature, always trying to impress one another with their half-baked "intellectualism," miss the point of life, which is to find and nurture simple, loving relationships. This is what Woody's character, Isaac Davis, has with Mariel Hemingway's Tracy. It is of course her youth—she's a high school senior—that assures her exemplary innocence and eventually assures the demise of their relationship. Which the movie deeply regrets.

Interestingly, in 1979 when *Manhattan* was released, people did not make much of the fact that Tracy was technically jailbait or of the disparity in age between the two lovers—a matter that has been the source of ever-increasing grumbles as Woody himself has grown older but still continues to have relationships with much younger women in his films (and, of course, in his marriage). In the case of *Manhattan,* the charm and handsomeness of the film (again shot by Willis)—particularly apparent in the completely unsniggering way Hemingway was presented (such a likable, guileless girl)—silenced criticism. In some ways *Manhattan* is one of Woody's trickiest films, morally speaking. But he got away with it, since at this point he was still operating within parameters acceptable to his audience.

Stardust Memories, as we've already seen, offered nothing of the sort. It looks weird from the outset; it has visibly lost touch with reality. Now, you could argue that Woody's early funny ones were, in their way, equally dreamlike. There is something distinctly surreal, for example, about *Bananas*—the way it jumps from place to place, from gag topic to gag topic. Everyone still remembers the absurdist intrusions of Howard

Cosell covering a revolution (and a sexual encounter) as if they were sporting events. But the movie is entirely free of subtext; it is just one damn thing after another. And thirty years ago people liked that purity. It was a little like listening to a Henny Youngman monologue—all jokes with minimal (at best, free-associational) transitions between them and no subjectivity whatsoever. Woody's character (as he was in all his early films) was a very simple type—a coward putting up a brave front, sexually voracious but essentially clueless around women. As Woody says, this figure owed more to Bob Hope's screen character than to anyone else, though the narrative context in which he appeared was even sketchier than Hope's.

With the exception of *Love and Death* (which has a bit more plot and, for Woody, an exotic setting, nineteenth-century Russia), these early movies, when you return to them now, are much less funny than they seemed at the time. Individual gags and sequences still make you laugh, but overall they make me at least feel restless, dissatisfied with their patchiness. But, of course, most moviegoers don't return to old movies. They operate on memory, and their memory of these movies is of youthful, nostalgically tinged hilarity. To reevaluate these movies now would be to reevaluate themselves. Better to go on trusting fond memory. And go on complaining about or ignoring something like *Stardust Memories*.

That's fine with Woody. And had his nature been different, he could, as we've already noted, gone on making gag comedies forever. He has a gift, amounting to a kind of genius, for concocting jokes—and not just verbal ones of the "he said—she said" variety. He has the ability, as well, to construct quite lengthy sequences, involving a fair amount of physical humor. As he says, his gift for gag writing appeared very early in life. He started making money writing jokes for newspaper columns when he was an adolescent, and moved on, when he was still a kid, to high-paying television gag-smithing. As he also says, this talent is a mystery to him; he compares it to natural, untutored gifts his schoolmates had, say, for drawing or carrying a tune.

Woody retains this ability. It's the way his mind naturally works. But it presents a problem to him, and to his audience. It's typical of people who have a natural talent for any form of human activity to undervalue it. Whether it is writing jokes or sonnets, what looks hard to the rest of us comes easy for them, and they feel they shouldn't take much—or maybe any— credit for it.

Instead they devote themselves to more effortful activities, work that requires discipline and struggle and involves them in comparisons—primarily in their own minds—with people whose own natural gifts they cannot match. And probably should not try to match. Woody, for example, will go to his grave disappointed that he never made a film that could be mentioned in the same breath with one of Bergman's.

In part that's because he cannot, for very long, stop writing gags. Yes, to be sure, he has made other, essentially humorless films (*September, Another Woman, Sweet and Lowdown*). But in truth his wisecracking impulse is near to irrepressible. Why that should confuse people is a mystery to me. Wit is intelligence's most trustworthy sign; ponderousness is its deadly enemy. But people like to keep things straight. They don't like humor's intrusion when they have signed on for a sober film or play or book. Or vice versa. In Woody's case, it reminds them of his former nonstop hilarity, but since the hilarity is now often less nonstop it makes them feel disappointed, even slightly cheated. C'mon Woody, make us fall down the way you used to.

4

About a year after I conducted my interview with him, Woody was on stage at the 92nd Street Y in New York, more or less bemoaning his congenital funniness. According to Sarah Boxer's *New York Times* report on the event, he had this to say about his largely thwarted ambitions: "I regret that my muse was a comic muse and not a dramatic muse. I would rather have had the gifts of Eugene O'Neill or Tennessee Williams than the gifts I got. I'm not kvetching. I'm glad I got any gifts at all. But I would like to do something great."

He went on to say: "I'm not overly humble. I feel I had grandiose plans for myself when I started out. And I have not lived up to them. I've done some things that are perfectly nice. But I had a much grander conception of where I should end up in the artistic firmament. What has made it doubly poignant for me is that I was never denied the opportunity. The only thing standing between me and greatness is me."

You can see how statements of this kind would annoy his public. In our interview Woody implies that laziness is a factor in what he perceives as his failure. He seems to be saying that if he had spent less time playing his clarinet or watching sports on television, he might have achieved more of what he wanted to. At the same time he specifically rejects the notion that he is a workaholic. That he is obviously—and without competition—the most prolific writer-director in modern cinematic history cuts no ice with him. He could have done more. He could still do more.

In that he does not work to the utter exclusion of all other activity or emotional traffic, he is probably not, clinically speaking, a workaholic. But considering that most of us truly are goof-offs, few heed his protestations of innocence. They also disbelieve his modesty about what he has accomplished. The criticism of my television show that I most often heard was of his casual dismissiveness of his own work. People just didn't believe that he likes maybe four of his thirty-two films. They thought he was having me on. Or maybe having himself on.

But I believe him. People as fecund as Woody are in touch with their own tirelessness, which is, like the ability to write gags, an inexplicable gift (or plague). It is just part of their being, and it never feels to them—whatever others may think—that they are overworking. Something similar can, I think, be said of their self-evaluations. A friend of mine—also a prolific writer—says we get to do only four or five things in life that are truly worthwhile, but that we only hesitantly acknowledge in public. The rest is just making a living. Or as Norman Mailer, another prodigious worker, once put it, running existential errands.

Most artists operate on a different schedule. Writing fewer books, making fewer movies, their products inevitably take on—not least in their own minds—a more burnished glow. Their fewer works must be more important because, proportionately, they have consumed more years, more (apparent) psychic effort.

I suppose we must admit the possibility that Woody's work might have been better had there been less of it or if more time had been spent on individual films. But don't count on it. His ratio of successes to failures is not worse than that of less productive artists. The mystery of creativity includes the mystery of pacing.

There is, as Woody says, another element motivating his ceaseless productivity—the therapeutic element. He creates and populates imaginary cinematic worlds—mostly better ones than he encounters in ordinary existence—in which he can escape his existential gloom. The women in this world are prettier, and everyone is wittier, their surroundings more agreeable, than they are in real life. Sometimes his films are period pieces, which permits him to escape contemporary life entirely.

How dare he complain about this opportunity when all the rest of us are permanently trapped in quotidian reality? How dare he complain when his work has given him a life of quite reasonable wealth and the privilege, whether he uses it or not, of free access to all the glamour and stir anyone could possibly want?

Perhaps this accounts for the general dismay over *Stardust Memories*. There's the Felliniesque dream train, filled with oddly garbed figures, many of them apparently drawn from Sandy's past life. There are the space aliens pooh-poohing his artistic ambitions and his *weltschmerz*. There are the unprepared-for appearances of all those figures clawing for his attention. There's a quite literal (and wistful) embrace of magic, with Sandy actually levitating a woman. This says nothing about the ending, in which almost all these characters gather, a la the conclusion of *8-1/2,* to confront him, but in a much less benign spirit than Fellini's people did.

It's clear why the audience reacted so dubiously. Where had their beloved funnyman gone? Or, perhaps more to the point, where was he going? Most immediately, he was seemingly going backward. *A Midsummer Night's Sex Comedy* was set in a country house around the turn of the nineteenth century, and though Woody has always denied the resemblance, you could see that it was, at least in mood and setting, not entirely unlike *Smiles of a Summer Night*. On the other hand, it was a typical Allen movie in that everyone present for this weekend was in love not with the partners they rode in with but with someone else in the house party. We also did not particularly notice that the film ended on a magical realist note—with Woody's character, a somewhat impractical inventor, having one of his creations actually work, putting the characters in touch with the unseen world. It is also, I think, a film that seems somewhat better—anyway, jollier—in retrospect than it did when it was released and turned out to be one of Woody's less successful box office attractions.

It was made virtually simultaneously with *Zelig,* which is, I think, a masterpiece. It takes the form of a mock documentary, and, as Woody says, when it was released press attention focused on the technical aspects of the production—basically getting newly shot film to match old newsreel material, or inserting Zelig into the old footage so that he seems to be relating to actual historical characters. All of this is superbly—all right, magically—managed. It is one of the great special-effects films in that the effects are all placed in the service of an idea instead of simply serving our desire for sensation.

But it is the film's underlying idea that is truly brilliant—the eponymous anti-hero being a man with no qualities, therefore able to fit himself in, at will, with the famous. Or with the anonymous. Naturally he himself becomes famous for this ability. Equally naturally, he succumbs to Nazism in its early days. Why not? The Nazis are, if anything, as famous (or as infamous) as all the other people with whom Zelig has ingratiated himself.

Woody says he was completely aware of this film's political implications. Fascism is a doctrine that appeals to people with no qualities, who need some ideology—even (perhaps particularly) a perverse and violent one—to complete themselves, with a ready-made set of "ideas" they can embrace. There is, as well, an aspect of the film that is closer to the main line, as I see it, of Woody's work. That is the way Zelig persistently confounds the rational world. In addition to its fake and doctored newsreel footage, the film contains a good bit of "scientific" footage—records of scientists testing Zelig, both physically and psychologically, as they attempt to discover his chimera's secrets. They always fail. Because he is a magical creature, entirely inexplicable to arrogant science. Or, for that matter, to the booming voice-over narrator of the "documentary" we are watching. Or to the real intellectuals (Irving Howe, Susan Sontag, Saul Bellow) who attempt, with comic ineptitude, to explain or at least to contextualize him socially.

In the end—and this is one of the factors that make *Zelig* perhaps the most fascinating of all Woody's films—Zelig must lose his magical abilities. Nazism is too dangerous for him to toy with. He must return to that reality we are all, alas, trapped within. It is love—Mia Farrow's psychiatrist spots him at a Nazi rally, and her signals to him from the crowd break through his dream state—that saves him. The two make an improbable escape from Hitler's Germany, and he settles back into normalcy—happily or not, we cannot be entirely certain. What we can be certain of is that *Zelig* is a superbly executed comic idea that makes a deft, sobering point about human behavior and the extremes of which it is capable.

Woody followed *Zelig* with *Broadway Danny Rose,* which gave him a chance to act a New York lowlife for the first time—a desperately small-time talent agent—and Mia Farrow the opportunity to play a mob moll. Woody liked the acting opportunity it provided him (for some reason he thinks he is, really, deep in his heart, sort of a Danny Rose *shlep*) as well as the chance to pay tribute to talent agents who loyally stick with their acts, then get fired when the acts make it to the big time. It was a genial and energetic little movie but not a huge reach for him.

Not, certainly, in comparison to his next release, *The Purple Rose of Cairo,* which is, like *Zelig,* a great film. And a devious one. You can read it simply as an amusing fantasy, in which a character steps down from the screen and into the life of Mia Farrow's downtrodden, depression-era hash-house waitress, briefly touching it with romance and glamour. You can also read it as a smart satire on the kind of silliness Hollywood routinely dished out in the 1930s and '40s.

The picture Farrow's Cecilia obsessively watches as she escapes the awfulness of her life is in fact called *The Purple Rose of Cairo,* and it shows bored New York show-biz swells taking a holiday in Egypt where they find Jeff Daniels's Tom Baxter in a tomb, searching for the eponymous flower. They whisk him back to New York for some high life—penthouses, white telephones, dry martinis. While in the midst of this improbable deliriousness he notices Cecilia in the audience, addresses her, and literally steps off the screen and into her reality. Eventually Daniels plays both a screen character and the actual movie star, Gil Shepherd, who is impersonating him.

It's all wonderfully befuddling. But, as Woody says, he did not intend simply to make idle fun of forgotten Hollywood genres. Or pay tribute to them. By using this marvelous cinematic device (first toyed with, less consequentially, by Buster

Keaton in *Sherlock, Jr.*) he was of course making one of his boldest magical-realistic assaults on his audience's expectations.

He was, to begin with, trying to draw a dramatic distinction between the repetitiveness of our fantasy lives, in which the projections of our desires appear and reappear with clockwork regularity, and reality's utter lack of predictability. At the same time he was saying that, for many people, reality does have a certain sameness—the dull job, the nasty marriage, the lack of hope that things can appreciably change—that requires escape into the ephemeral palliatives of mechanized fantasy. For a movie critically to take up the subtext offered by all escapist movies (and there is hardly any other kind) is truly original, indeed unprecedented as far as I know. Most movies about the movies are either giddy with nostalgia or grim with star-is-born melodrama. *The Purple Rose of Cairo* alone tries to address the most basic way the medium works on us.

This is not to say that it is unfunny. The film within the film is a good satire on old-fashioned program picture-making. The consternation of the on-screen characters when one of their number deserts the screen and enters the auditorium is lovely to behold. As the guardians of fantasy's regularity, they are deeply upset when its predictability deserts them. And all that aside, Farrow and Daniels are superb in their roles.

But in the end *Purple Rose* comes close to tragedy. It leaves a crushed Cecilia right where she started, as a movie fan, looking up at the screen for her daily dose of fantasy. She is bereft of friends and family—the latter probably a good thing, since her husband is a vulgar and sadistic man—and of imaginative resources, other than those her neighborhood theater provides with each change of its bill. As Woody says, she made the right choice; one cannot live sanely within a fantasy world. He seemed to imply, in our interview, that having made the correct choice Cecilia might make others that would lead her into a somewhat better life, though I don't think he entertains high hopes in that regard.

But no matter. *The Purple Rose of Cairo* is a perfectly judged movie. It veers neither too far toward satire nor toward the tragic. Its tone is wryly compassionate. The proportion of magic to realism remains in haunting balance. And it is a movie that even Woody continues to think came out well, by which, as he makes clear in our interview, he means that in his judgment he effectively realized on screen what he envisioned when he was writing the script.

5

Although *Hannah and Her Sisters* is the most commercially successful of all his movies, Woody does not short-list it among his personal favorites. And I agree with him for reasons I cannot entirely fathom. It is a handsome and well-acted film, and it contains what is, for him, a significant structural innovation to which he would return in later years—weaving together two related but nevertheless distinct story lines, one of them largely comic, the other largely sober.

In the former, Woody's character, Mickey Sachs, is a television producer who suddenly loses his hearing, which an extensively consulted medical profession thinks may be the symptom of a potentially fatal brain tumor (actually it is the result of sitting too close, too long, to a rock band). This confrontation with mortality—always a subject of prime interest to Woody—is managed with huge comic aplomb. In the other story, Michael Caine's Elliot, a fashionable money manager, is married to the eponymous Hannah but lusts after her sister, Lee, who in turn is married to a choleric painter (Max von Sydow), and enters into a guilt-ridden affair with her. Woody, as he admits, is drawn to sisterly relationships—lots of dramatic tension there—and he also intended this aspect of his film to come to an ending bleaker than he finally provided. The marginally happier ending he settled on was largely responsible for *Hannah*'s large—by Woody's standards—commercial success.

I cannot say why I didn't fully join this film's chorus of approval. It certainly remains an enjoyably watchable movie. Maybe it's because the film is, finally, too easy on its principals, lets them elide—not quite with a shrug, but close to one—the darker issues of loyalty and trust that haunt and erratically move them. They don't quite come to grips with them in a fully consequential manner.

Radio Days is a much less imposing movie—a seemingly slight memory piece—but it is, in my estimation, one of

Woody's best and most delicate works. He is, like many a novelist (and very few filmmakers), a sneaky autobiographer. There are disguised aspects of his personal history in many of his films. No, his family did not live in ear-shattering proximity to the thundering Coney Island roller coaster, as he portrayed them in the famous *Annie Hall* childhood flashback. But their little Brooklyn house did, apparently, resound with quarrelsome racket. So, metaphorically, its portrayal in this film is accurate. Similarly, as a kid Woody loved doing magic tricks and did perform them in public, as Sandy does in one of the *Stardust Memories* flashbacks.

Radio Days is his most extended rumination on his childhood, and it contains incidents from his life—his first trip to Radio City Music Hall and his exploration of an exhibition of war materiel nearby. His father was for a time a cab driver, as the father in *Radio Days* is. And the family did at various times live near Brooklyn's Atlantic shore. Most important, though, is the relationship between this unnamed family and their favorite radio programs.

If you were a child growing up in the 1940s, this connection with these fictional voices, invading your home on a regularly scheduled basis, was a significant one. They brought a touch of glamour and adventure to our little boyish and necessarily humdrum lives. They bent and scored us just as the movies Woody satirized in *Purple Rose* did. He recognizes that their fantasies posed a certain danger to us (not morally but perhaps in the way they predisposed some part of our sensibilities to more or less permanent infantilization), yet he treats them with wry affection in his film.

More important, he sympathetically imagines a life for the people who became the stars of this relatively short-lived medium. They are genial, happy to be welcomed to the best restaurant tables, a little bit randy in part because they so enjoy their rather innocent and relatively minor celebrity. Indeed, there is something childlike in their behavior, which analogizes nicely to the childlike delight of their listeners. The movie is perfectly pitched in this respect; it shows the not inconsequential impact of radio on people's lives at the time, but it is equally aware of its ephemeral nature.

Or maybe one should say its magical nature. The medium was based, of course, on scientific principles that were—a few science geeks aside—obscure to most of us. What was interesting was the way radio worked on us, how a few actors, grouped around a microphone, reading script pages, and abetted only by a small orchestra and a sound-effects man, could create entirely persuasive alternative universes with minimal means. They put pictures into our heads. And there was often a vast discontinuity between the way these players really looked and the impressions they created.

Woody has fun with this, particularly with the casting of short, round, balding Wallace Shawn as a radio superhero. He also, I think, draws an implicit analogy between the magical worlds they created and Manhattan as it appeared to his wondering small boy's eyes in the 1940s. The city the radio stars inhabit glows with a glamour and a promise that is almost mythic.

Woody is entirely aware that the city is not quite as it first appeared to his bedazzled little self. He is aware of his own youthful provinciality. Yet his affection for this partly imagined city has never wavered. He is, naturally, aware of all the damage that has been done to it over the years, yet clings to his belief that its magic is impermeable. If he has a public cause that always attracts his support, it is the city. He has made short films about it for various charities. He makes public appearances in support of urban preservation projects. And, most important, he presents an image of New York in his films that keeps its allure alive for newer generations.

Interestingly, *Radio Days* prefigures one of the losses the city would suffer in the postwar years. New York was the center of radio broadcasting from the medium's beginnings, the home of legendary voices and programs, despite the rise in the late thirties and the forties of Los Angeles as a competitor. Radio was, or seemed, central to New York's glamorous image. There were always stories in the press about particularly popular radio personalities with cabs waiting for them at one studio to take them on to another one on a split-second schedule so that they could play a different character on a different show. There were pictures of these figures dining and dancing and generally leading exciting lives in Big Town (to borrow the title of a radio newspaper drama). It must have seemed to many in radio that the Manhattan Merry-Go-Round would never stop spinning.

But at the end of Woody's film the radio personalities, having gathered for New Year's Eve dinner in a hotel restaurant, troop up to the roof to see out the old year and see in the new one. The electric signs of Broadway stretch out before them, and optimism is in the air. Once the moment passes, they head back down the stairs as Shawn's character reflects on the ephemeral nature not just of radio but—this being a Woody Allen film—of existence. It is brief, lightly managed, *sotto voce* monologue. But the film's heart and meaning is contained in it. This is the way worlds end, with a whisper. Not a word is said about television being just around the corner. Or about the wrecker's balls that would ultimately transform Times Square into something unrecognizable. Or those changes in fashion and prevailing preoccupations that would render Woody's more gracious New York an historical artifact.

If Shawn's fears of the future are whispered, it must be said that *Radio Days* was probably, for most viewers, a wisp of a film—short, pretty, amusing, episodic, "unimportant."

But that does not quite discourage me from thinking that this is one of Woody's most accomplished movies, one which takes up, very lightly and gracefully, some of his most abiding themes—his somewhat unreasoned (but heartfelt) love of his city, his sense of the endless mutability of fashion, his awareness of how magical phenomena, like radio, can profoundly affect us and then, in the wink of history's eye, become totally irrelevant.

It also represents his most direct confrontation with his

own ethnicity. Woody is, of course, Jewish by birth, and in his screen appearances he has never attempted to pass as anything else. He is ever a "New Yorker" (to borrow the code word many American outlanders use to identify Jews). Mostly the occupations of his characters are "Jewish"—television writers and producers, for example. Occasionally he speaks or allows himself to be seen as explicitly Jewish. One thinks of the famous comic cut in *Annie Hall* where the heroine's wildly prejudiced "Grammy" glances across the ham the Halls are sharing with Alvy at dinner and sees him in full Hasidic dress and beard. In *Deconstructing Harry* he argues religion with his brother-in-law, who is a late-life convert to strict orthodoxy. I think his *Zelig* character—with his rootlessness and uncanny skill at adapting to changing circumstances—can be read as a projection of, or comment on, Jewish adaptability. The near-fatal victimization of his clerk character in *Shadows and Fog* can be seen as another aspect of Jewishness.

But, like Zelig, he is not explicitly identified as Jewish. And the same is true of the *Radio Days* family. They "look" Jewish, and in their passionate disputations they "act" Jewish. (Well, anyway, they are assuredly not button-down WASPs.) But nothing is directly made of their ethnicity. It is something we can deal with or not. And Woody simply presents it, almost objectively.

I have no way of knowing what age Woody was when he rejected God or his faith. What we do know is that he came of age in the 1950s and '60s, when ethnic comedy was at a deep discount in American popular culture. As early as 1952 an article in the Jewish intellectual journal *Commentary* had lamented the "vanishing" Jew in comedy and elsewhere. The dialect comedians of vaudeville were now gone. Groucho— one of Woody's favorites—was now the deracinated wise-cracker of television's *You Bet Your Life.* Mort Sahl, who played a mentoring role in Woody's stand-up years, was also deeply admired by Woody, but his comedy, based largely on current events, was not ethnic. And then, of course, there was the aforementioned Bob Hope, a distinctly WASP idol for Woody.

In other words, even if he had been so inclined, there was no specifically Jewish comedian around for him to model his early comic character on. His routines, like his films-to-be, tended to stress New York inconvenience, and probably a lot of us vaguely understood that some 50 percent of America's Jews lived in the metropolis and thus could draw our own conclusions about the ultimate source of Woody's point of view. Nonetheless he never mentioned it. Later, in the sixties, when he began making movies, other filmmakers were stressing what J. Hoberman has called "bad boy" Jewish angst, in movies like *Goodbye, Columbus,* but Woody's character, as angst-ridden as anyone, never traced his frustrations, romantic or otherwise, to his Jewishness. He would occasionally play more "Jewish" than at other times (*Broadway Danny Rose* is a good example), but he never mentioned this choice in his scripts.

I have to ask myself, as a WASP, if that was part of his appeal to me. Drawn into his milieu as I was—I went to psychiatrists too in those days—did I in some subliminal way appreciate his universalizing of the urban life? I suspect I did. Did the fact that my social and professional life revolved almost exclusively around Jews who, like Woody, were largely acculturated, neither stressing nor denying their ethnic pasts, increase my affection for his work? I suspect it did. We had not yet arrived at *Seinfeld,* the Jewishness of which was almost entirely expressed in the ironic, Talmudic examination of trivial incidents, but we were heading there, and Woody's work was part of that unspoken process.

<h1 style="text-align:center">6</h1>

The movies Woody made immediately after *Radio Days* were among his most morally serious works. I have little to say about *September,* which I suspect Woody thinks more highly of than most of us do. It's a chamber piece—more people in a country house, lusting after the wrong partners—and it was for him perhaps his most difficult production—much recasting and reshooting. But it went largely unseen, even though his direction was very assured. Perhaps the hardest thing to do directorially is to be interesting with a small cast in a tight place—linking the shoots gracefully, keeping the geography of the scenes clear for the audience—and this he did silkily. Even so, the movie remains inconsequential for me, nowhere near as intense or aspiring as *Interiors,* which is its natural analogy.

There's nothing inconsequential about *Another Woman*. It contains a great performance by Gena Rowlands, playing a chilly philosophy professor, and a very novel plot device. Rowlands's Marion sublets a quiet apartment in order to work on her new book. But she is interrupted by the psychoanalytic sessions of a young, pregnant woman (Mia Farrow), whose angst accidentally leaks into Marion's retreat via the hot-air registers in the apartment's heating system. Something about the younger woman's near-anarchical troubles touches Rowlands's character, and she begins reexamining her own cold life—her sterile marriage, the abstractness of her intellectual life, her relationship with her professor father who has also devoted himself to scholarship at the expense of emotional warmth, her brother who is even more damaged than she is.

In this film Woody takes up, most directly, the issue he began exploring in *Annie Hall* and *Manhattan*—the ways in which very bright and articulate people avoid emotional involvement by devoting themselves to ideas—to opinion-making and opinion-mongering. He is very good on this subject, and, in a way, very brave on it, for if he has a core American audience the people of this class are at its center. They do not pay their money to be affronted.

That said, it must be added that *Another Woman* is somewhat undone by the fact that its self-absorbed and entirely humorless characters tend to push us away from the kind of involvement we want to experience at the movies. This is somewhat mitigated by Rowlands's subtle playing. She believes she is a warm and caring figure and is dismayed to discover that other people—aside from a stepdaughter with whom she exhibits genuine warmth—do not see her so. Still . . . the movie is easy to admire and hard to like.

Woody briefly relaxed the didactic pressure with his contribution to the anthology film *New York Stories,* which was entitled "Oedipus Wrecks." It took him back to territory more familiar to his audience. He plays a character bedeviled by the Jewish Mother from Hell, who disappears when she volunteers for a magician's act and then reappears in the skies over Manhattan, advising her son (played by Woody) about his love life and drawing the whole town into their drama. It's a funny little piece—talk about magic realism—as neatly worked out as an old-fashioned TV sketch. But surely it did nothing to prepare anyone for the high moral tone of *Crimes and Misdemeanors.*

In talking about that film Woody uttered my favorite sentence of our interview: "I just wanted to illustrate, in an entertaining way, that there's no God. . . ." The remark is unconsciously funny (Woody Allen is almost never consciously funny when he's discussing his work), one of those things that just slip out when you're concentrating hard on a subject, not completely minding your p's and q's.

On the other hand, it pretty well sums up *Crimes and Misdemeanors.* The fashionable eye surgeon Judah (Martin Landau) has a mistress, Dolores (Anjelica Huston), who is impatient for him to do as he has long promised—divorce his wife and marry her. But she's a vulgar sort, not at all the kind of person he could introduce to his chic friends. He would happily pay her off, but that doesn't interest her. If Judah will not marry her, she will pull down his perfect life and leave him standing in its wreckage.

As she becomes more and more threatening, the thought of disposing of her becomes more and more attractive. Judah has a mobbed-up brother who can arrange the hit, which he accomplishes almost as a routine errand. Judah suffers pangs of guilt. He is nervous about the detective who comes sniffing around. But for the cop it's a minor case—he has a lot on his plate—and soon Judah's guilt subsides and he glides smoothly back into the even tenor of his well-appointed life.

Among Judah's patients is a man of perfect goodness, a rabbi named Ben, played by Sam Waterston, serenely certain that we live in a morally ordered universe. On the other hand, Ben is going blind. Which proves that good deeds—good lives—never go unpunished as surely as Judah's criminal life proves the opposite.

If this were all there was to *Crimes and Misdemeanors* it would be a very rich film. But there is more, namely Woody's Cliff, a comically earnest documentary filmmaker, whose brother-in-law, Lester (Alan Alda), is everything he's not—a shrewd, pompous, egocentric, and wildly successful producer of television sitcoms. As is so often the case with such figures, the world has begun to take him seriously—he has recently guest-lectured on comedy at Harvard, retailing his pretentious theories on what makes us laugh. He hires Cliff to make

a PBS documentary about him, a job the latter takes in order
to finance his own film about a great philosopher who is also a
Holocaust survivor.

Cliff is not a particularly good man. Or a particularly bad
one. He is our surrogate in the film in that he more or less
means well and is doing his best to survive in a world that
keeps presenting him with ambiguous moral choices. His wife
is contemptuous of his pure intentions—justifiably so, since he
takes a shine to Hillary, an equally sober PBS functionary,
played by Mia Farrow. In the end he is—next to Dolores—the
person most victimized in the film. His philosopher-subject,
despite the life-affirming statements we see him making in
Cliff's footage, inexplicably commits suicide. Hillary succumbs to Lester's wiles, and Cliff himself is fired from Lester's
documentary when he starts intercutting footage of his subject
with noxious dictators.

This film, like *Hannah,* is bifurcated—essentially inter-
twining two major narrative streams that are contradictory in
mood. What holds it together is a metaphor: eyes. It is about
the ways we see and don't see, morally speaking. There is
Judah's profession to begin with and the tragedy that befalls
his patient, Ben. Early in the film Dolores makes the standard
observation about eyes being the windows of the soul, which
Judah ignores. His view of such matters is scientific and materialistic. But when he sees Dolores dead and stares into her
sightless eyes, their blankness makes a profound impression
on him. We may debate the existence of the soul; we cannot

debate the terror we feel at the absence of life, even a life that is not a particularly good one.

But Woody's metaphor extends well beyond that moment. The impossible Lester must convert every experience into a bad joke. Cliff is his opposite; he cannot tolerate a joke, most especially the cosmic one that robs him of his saintly subject before he has finished his film about him. He has been seeing him intently through his viewfinder, but he has not seen into his despair. So he and his brother-in-law are each only partially sighted. And it is interesting that Ben, who is actually going blind, is already blind to the iniquities of the world. Were he not, one imagines, he could not be quite so comfortably good.

Woody likes the figure of Ben. He has said that he envies him his sustaining faith. He believes he is one of the two characters in the film who "triumph." (The other is Cliff's niece, whom he adores, and who is, because of her youth, still an innocent; whether, like Ben, she can sustain that state as she grows older and more experienced is an open question and one Woody does not address.)

But finally this movie is not, most significantly, about guilt and innocence. It may be, as Woody says, about the absence of God in the universe. But that's just another way of saying that the universe is silent and indifferent to what we do in it. In a world ruled by chance, more than likely you can get away with murder. It is also true, as Woody says, that good intentions actually mean as little as bad intentions as we go through life. All that really counts is success—getting money, rising in class, which in turn will make you famous. Which, naturally, increases your power to do as you please, without fear of condemnation, either to jail or to pariah status.

On balance it could be argued that *Crimes and Misdemeanors* is the most successful of Woody's more overtly serious films. In part that's because it is leavened by the *spritzing* that goes on in the Cliff story. More important, though, is the sheer liveliness of the storytelling and the characterizations in both parts of the film. There are no dull incidents and no dull people here—they have in their admittedly misguided passions a heat that is missing, say, from the principal figures of *Interiors* or *September* or *Another Woman,* and this energy disguises the rather schematic nature of the picture's moral reflections. In short, it "works" better for audiences than some of Woody's other highly aspiring films. It seems to have caught in their minds better too. People appear to remember it more vividly than they do many of his other works.

7

Woody's next two films, *Alice* and *Shadows and Fog,* represent a decisive return to magic realism. The first of them is controlled by an embrace of this manner more wholehearted than in any of his films since *Stardust Memories.* Indeed, it is the central element of a plot in which the eponymous central figure (Mia Farrow) is presented as a standard upper-class Manhattan housewife, trapped in a boring marriage with a husband who cheats, her restlessness unsalved by the usual escapes (shopping, the beauty salon). One day she goes to a comically cranky Chinese herbalist (Keye Luke, in his last movie performance). She thinks of him as a purveyor of simple yet exotic solutions to existential symptomology (like health food or acupuncture). But he presents her with potions by which she can render herself invisible, fly through the skies, return backward in time.

Nowhere in Woody's body of work is the possibility of magical transformation so starkly (and therefore humorously) presented. Bang! A banal and quotidian life becomes one of miracles and wonders. It's quite funny. And Alice does not stop with routine revenges on her clueless husband—she embarks on an affair with a sweet-spirited jazz player, Joe (Joe Mantegna), whom she meets at her child's school. At the end of the film she has put all material comforts aside and joined Mother Teresa in India.

The movie is very simple in spirit. The problems it presents are commonplace among Alice's class; its magical solutions (invisibility, flight) are of the sort that children dream of embracing; its denouement (joining Mother Teresa in her life of poverty and good works) one of the simpy clichés of late-twentieth-century pop spirituality. It feels like a satire on the common modernist yearnings for an escape from complexity and materialist dissatisfaction. And maybe, in part, it is.

But Woody's atheism has always been of the disappointed kind. In interviews he has often expressed his wish for some persuasive alternative to the Godless universe. (His character in *Hannah* is seen to be on just such a quest, albeit a hilariously disappointed one.) *Alice* is an expression of his desire for moral and spiritual order, which he knows is childlike and which he presents in almost cartoonish terms in the film. It is perhaps a minor work, but there is a nice tossed-off air about the film-making, particularly in its very simply accomplished special effects, that makes it attractive.

In contrast, *Shadows and Fog* announces the seriousness of its intention from its first frame. It is a black-and-white film, shot in the manner of European expressionist silent films—lots of backlight and fairly radical camera angles. Set in a mythical Mittel Europa in the earlier twentieth century, it presents Woody's central character, Kleinmann, as a clerk, awakened in the middle of the night to join a posse searching for a serial killer. Before dawn, Kleinmann encounters most of the ways in which we fail to contain monstrousness: science tries to study the killer but cannot comprehend or explain his apparently motiveless malignity; conventional politics is represented by the searching citizenry, including the befuddled police, all of whom are constantly misled and are, in any case, prone to hysteria; art is represented by a circus, whose owner-star (John Malkovich) strikes grandiose poses but is pompously irrelevant to the case's solution. A whorehouse, of course, represents pure escape, but the hedonism on offer there is more cynical than palliative.

What we are talking about here is, I think, a metaphor for the Holocaust. That is to say, we are being presented with an evil unprecedented in the experience of a rationally organized community. And we are seeing that conventional solutions to evil on a grand scale are doomed to failure. At the end of the picture the killer is stalking Kleinmann, who retreats to the circus ground. There a magician awaits him, standing on the far side of a magical mirror. This figure urges Kleinmann to jump through the glass, make his escape to its far, mystical side. Kleinmann does not believe this is possible, but as the menacing figure advances on him, it becomes his last hope. He makes the leap and, lo, he is safe. The last we see of him he is making childish—relieved—faces at the killer.

Does Woody really believe that magic can save us from events like the Holocaust (or, for that matter, from Al Qaeda)? No, of course he doesn't. He is not a mystic. Or a nut case. He is simply a man who knows how desperately we desire release from our woes. It may or may not be that Alice, for example, finds surcease from her pain in serving the cause of painfully self-conscious Goodness. It may or may not be that Kleinmann will find happiness on the far side of the mirror. Both "solutions" are, finally, fantasies—available in the movies but not in real life.

8

After *Alice* and *Shadows and Fog,* Woody largely abandoned magic realism. None of his subsequent films overtly traffics in otherworldly interventions in ordinary lives. There are, to be sure, odd strokes of the kind we've already mentioned in *Mighty Aphrodite* and *Deconstructing Harry* (and the magical dance at the end of *Everyone Says I Love You,* which defies reality's physics). But these are mere gestures, not the true substance of these movies. What's best and most memorable about *Everyone Says I Love You* is the cast repeatedly bursting into croaking song on New York's streets and other locations. These sequences evoke and also neatly parody the truly magical (and entirely improbable) perfection achieved by the singers and dancers in similar circumstances in traditional musicals. They are affectionate and effective satires on a more conventional kind of movie "magic."

But Woody's movies from 1992 onward are, in the main, grounded very firmly in reality. Or, anyway, reality as Woody perceives it. Nevertheless his departure from convention in *Husbands and Wives* was a radical one, stylistically speaking. To be sure, we were back in the world of upper-middle-class misalliances. But for the moment Woody abandoned the manner he had evolved over the previous decade, which was based on very long takes, covered by a sinuously moving camera.

This is a style that simultaneously rewards and challenges his actors. On the practical level, it requires as much as a full day of camera rehearsal to prepare a single sequence. Once that's set, the actors are asked to do as many as ten pages of dialogue in a single take. This in turn requires them to memorize many more words than they are used to having in mind for the typical shot, reverse-shot movie sequence. On the other hand, it permits them to develop the nuances of their characters' behavior in more detail than usual. It may also contribute to the emotional intensity of the sequence. For the spectator, this method has the effect of drawing us smoothly, without jarring cuts, into the action.

In *Husbands and Wives,* as Woody says, he reversed all that. He didn't care, as he puts it, about film school "niceties." Most of his coverage was hand held, and he didn't care about jump cuts, or whether his left-to-rights (gaze meeting gaze smoothly) were correct. The result was a deliberately "nervous" film (think Godard, for whom he worked in 1987), puzzling and annoying to some critics and spectators. But as Woody also says, he felt this visual rawness was appropriate to a story full of emotional rawness—particularly in Judy Davis's great performance as a woman driven crazy by her husband's defection to a gorgeous personal-trainer/airhead. In any case, it energized a story that at heart is a typical Allenesque study of sexual betrayal—make that anarchy—among the privileged classes. (Sidney Pollack, the director, who appeared as Davis's wandering husband, has a scene where his new lover makes him nuts at a party and they storm out to his car, which he slams backward and forward into other cars, crumpling fenders in the process, as he tries to make a hasty exit. When the scene was done, he once told me, Woody murmured to him that that was more action than he had ever put into one of his movies, which is only arguably true but is certainly a signature of *Husbands and Wives.*)

Woody followed it with the minor *Manhattan Murder*

Mystery, which began production as he and Mia Farrow began their very public and acrimonious breakup (his former lover and lifelong pal, Diane Keaton, replaced her as the female lead). What is perhaps most notable about the film is that Woody hesitated to make it, as he told another interviewer, Stig Bjorkman, for a dozen years—a time span comparable to those that intervened between the writing and the making of those other modest comedies, *Small-time Crooks* and *Curse of the Jade Scorpion.* He just doesn't feel right about making movies so entirely lacking in weight. On the other hand, he obviously feels even less right about missing his annual release—using that word in two ways.

But in his most significant films of the nineties Woody radically shifted his emphasis. As our interview makes clear, he is a "huge" believer in the way chance—sheer dumb luck, being in the right place at the right time or vice versa—shapes our destinies. He also believes that it is the most important factor in the distribution of talent. We cannot, he strongly implies, take any credit for the manner in which gifts are—and are not—doled out to people at birth. We can, he says, learn some tricks of whatever trade fate imposes on us—discovering how to manage long takes gracefully might be one example—and we are obliged, of course, to show up and give it a go when a likely opportunity is on offer. But beyond that . . . success or failure, fame and fortune, is pretty much a matter of how the cards fall.

This is the theme of *Bullets over Broadway, Mighty*

Aphrodite, and *Celebrity.* Woody wrote the former with a new collaborator, Douglas McGrath. But one has to believe that its existential implication is largely Woody's—or at least that it is a topic he and McGrath came to agree upon. In it we find a depression-era playwright, David Shayne (John Cusack), struggling to get his latest effort mounted. He is a sometimes annoyingly pretentious young man and a deeply serious student of the drama. He knows its history. He knows everything about structuring a play—how to intertwine its characters, where to place the dramatic climaxes. He also believes that his previous works have been compromised by inept direction and wants to handle that job himself.

His immediate problem is money. His devoted producer (Jack Warden) is having trouble raising it amidst the downturn. He finally gets mob backing—in return for giving the boss's moll a part in the play. A guy named Cheech (Chazz Palminteri) comes along as her bodyguard. David's larger problem is that despite knowing all there is to know about playwriting, he lacks real gift—call it inspiration—for his self-appointed calling. Curiously, the uneducated, murderous Cheech has exactly what David is missing—perhaps we had better call it genius.

Cheech starts interrupting rehearsals with his suggestions. Soon enough he and David are meeting secretly and Cheech has his pencil out, doing the rewrites. To his credit, David recognizes, is even awed by, Cheech's raw talent. Naturally, the latter becomes proprietary about the work—to the extent that he rubs out the moll, whose performance is preventing the work from achieving its true stature. As a result, he is himself offed by the mob, but the play is a success.

Woody weaves what is, to my eye, one of his richest social textures in this movie. There's Dianne Wiest's superbly comic turn as an old-fashioned theatrical diva (with whom David falls into awed love). And there's Jim Broadbent's slyer but equally funny matinee idol, whose performance anxiety takes the form of gourmandizing, so that he balloons to ridiculous weight. The film as a whole is a not entirely unaffectionate satire on the kind of broadly posing theatricality—think Katherine Cornell or even Tallulah Bankhead—that the grimmer manner of method acting has largely supplanted. It is also a tribute—though more inferential than *Radio Days*—to certain aspects of old New York as Woody first encountered it.

All of that helps to make *Bullets over Broadway* a particularly delicious movie, both elegantly finished and unpredictably funny. It also serves to disguise its serious intent—the notion that however much you may desire greatness in your field, however much you may be willing to sacrifice to attain it, the luck of the genetic draw may—very likely will—frustrate you. You can, of course, entirely ignore this message (most of the reviewers did) and allow yourself to be absorbed in the burbling comic flow of the movie. But it is the ground on which this truly marvelous film is built, whether you choose to notice it or not.

Mighty Aphrodite was also a study in life's chanciness, but in some ways a simpler and more straightforward one, revolving as it does around Lenny played by Woody, obsessively worrying—it's why that Greek chorus is consulted—over whether or not he may have fathered a child with Mira Sorvino's Linda Ash (known professionally as Judy Cum), a delirious hooker he visits and befriends. It is a very light comedy, resolved—appropriately enough, given its Grecian motifs, by the descent of a quite literal *deus ex machina.* You might say that with this film Woody traces "magic realism" to its beginnings in dramatic history.

Deconstructing Harry is altogether a much rougher proposition. Stylistically it has some of the unfinished quality of *Husbands and Wives*—with Judy Davis again contributing one of her desperately loony performances as a wife betrayed not only sexually but in the pages of Harry Bloch's (the name is telling) tell-all novel. Which is to say that the picture again projects Woody back into the realm of marital betrayals. It is, as well, as full of flashbacks as *Stardust Memories.* This time, though, some of the characters step out of the past in order directly to address Harry in the present, which basically finds him heading to his old college, from which he dropped out, to receive some sort of academic award for his fiction. He is accompanied by his son, whom he abducts from his disagreeable mother (a wish-fulfillment for Woody, barred by court order from seeing his own son alone?), by another good-natured hooker, not unlike Mira Sorvino's *Aphrodite* whore (what, if anything, do these characters say about his feelings regarding sexual relations of the unpaid variety?), and by a friend who quietly dies as they roll along (talk about chance!). Along the way, in both memory and reality, Harry encounters members of his essentially dysfunctional family, some of whom are sexually involved with in-laws. Obviously this echoes, but with much more rawness, some of the themes of *Hannah and Her Sisters,* though his blunt rejection of conventional religious belief in a conversation with his pious brother-in-law is new; Woody has never spoken his atheism as scathingly as he does here.

In all, this may be the most complexly structured of all Woody's movies since *Stardust Memories.* But that's not the first thing you notice about the film. What you notice is the language—a stream of obscenities, quite unlike Woody's customary manner of address. It is something of a shock, especially since the picture appeared as Woody's custody fight with Mia Farrow—complete with her charges that he sexually abused his daughter—reached its tabloid heights. Indeed, the figure he played was as far as it was possible to get from the stammering, hesitant, overthinking, underperforming character that his audience had once loved. His Harry was a solipsist, totally self-involved, totally heedless of anyone else's interests, and essentially unlovable.

There was nothing coincidental about that. Or so I believe. I think he was flinging this figure into the face of his bad publicity. I think its bad language reflected Woody's own, largely impotent rage at the situation in which he found himself. I think, most of all, that its deliberate charmlessness—it simply refuses to insinuate itself with the audience—was

meant to challenge his audience, which for the most part refused the challenge.

The same occurred with *Celebrity*. David Thomson thinks
it "close to a really novel and brave scrutiny of modern reputa-
tion," and I agree with him. What's particularly interesting is
the twinning that occurs in it. Kenneth Branagh's Lee Simon,
a writer of vacuous celebrity profiles, aspires to higher
things—novels and screenplays—and shamelessly uses his
journalistic contacts to advance his more "serious" agenda. He
tries to hide his desperation, but you can almost smell the
sweat of it. He is also a shameless sexual adventurer.

He has a wife, Robin (Judy Davis), who is his opposite—
neurotically withdrawn, without ambition. Shattered by their
separation, she goes on a religious retreat, then visits a plastic
surgeon who has himself become a celebrity as a result of his
expert makeovers—as usual, Woody is making despairing fun
of the ways we try to transform ourselves. At the doctor's she
encounters a genuinely nice guy, Joe Mantegna's TV producer,
Tony Gardella, who uncomplicatedly offers her both love and
work. The former she embraces, then rejects, then finally
reembraces. The latter she ditheringly, at first incompetently,
tries. But she turns out to be good at it—a perfect audience
surrogate as she nervously interviews the rich and famous on
TV. In the process of so doing she herself becomes—what
else?—rich and famous. And fulfilled.

Meantime Branagh's character, constantly humiliated in
his pursuit of glamour and success, pulls himself together
enough to write a novel. But unable to remain faithful, he

abandons a good (and beautiful) woman, Famke Janssen's Bonnie, for Winona Ryder's neurotically manipulative and self-centered actress. When Bonnie finds out, she scatters his one hope of salvation, the only copy of Lee's manuscript, into New York's harbor. He later discovers that his idea has, in any case, been stolen by a more famous author (it's a form of *droit du seigneur*). At the end of the film Lee and Robin meet at a premiere. She's the toast of the town. He's the same loser he was when we first met him. Her last words to him? "I hope you catch a break."

Which is what the movie is about—catching or not catching a break. Or, to put it another way, being lucky or not lucky in your life. This is perhaps Woody's clearest statement of this perpetual theme of his. And it occurs in a film of great novelty yet one that explores anew the posings and posturings of the urban chattering classes.

It did him little good. For some reason the reviewers and the public fixated on Branagh's perfect imitation of Woody's typical on-screen manner—his stammerings and hesitations. It was perhaps a directorial mistake on Woody's part. We all knew that fifteen or twenty years earlier he would have been playing this part. Indeed, he could have—stretching our credulity a bit—played it in *Celebrity*. That he didn't bespeaks a desire, I think, to avoid the confused responses *Stardust Memories* provoked. On the other hand, having gone to this trouble, he probably should have urged Branagh to find a different manner.

But that does not seem to me a fatal flaw. Indeed, there's

often something weirdly funny in Branagh's line readings (the possibility that they may have amused Woody as well cannot be discounted). Especially when you take into account the savageness of the satire on our celebrity follies, it seems almost perverse not to read this film a little more closely and, if not sympathetically (on the whole, there are really only two fully likable characters in the piece), then as a smart and salutary comment on one of the ways we live now.

Perhaps needless to say, America likes its celebrity drama more sentimental. It wants to believe that its chosen ones are nice guys and gals, hard workers who deserve their fame and success. It likes to believe that when things go wrong—addictions, failed romances and marriages—adversity will, in short order, be banished by resort to a twelve-step program. It certainly does not want to believe that this dream public life may have a dark side. Or that privileged status is essentially unearned. In this particular case I think the public may have seen the picture as at least an inferential comment on Woody's own recent bout with the dark side of celebrity journalism.

Since *Celebrity,* Woody has retreated into something like inconsequence. *Sweet and Lowdown,* a study of a mean-spirited jazz musician—no folks, genius is no guarantee of good behavior—to me felt unfinished, almost hasty. There are some sweet moments in *Small-time Crooks* (mostly supplied by Elaine May's radical innocence), none at all in *Curse of the Jade Scorpion,* which is not very magical about hypnotism and not really the *film noir* satire it seems sometimes to aspire to being.

Hollywood Ending, I thought—almost alone—was much better, a fully worked-out comedy with a good central gimmick (the psychosomatically blinded director who must hide his condition and direct a movie sightlessly), rather good-natured satirical shafts aimed at Hollywood, a delicious performance by Mark Rydell as an eagerly loyal agent, and some excellent physical comedy by Woody (who is better in that area than he thinks he is). It even has a nice autobiographical touch—the film he makes is excoriated in the United States, but is hailed in France.

Still, we are not talking *The Purple Rose of Cairo* here. *Hollywood Ending* is just an agreeable little film, one for which Woody harbored fonder than usual commercial hopes that were disappointed in the domestic marketplace.

9

Which leaves him . . . where? Not exactly nowhere. As long as his European market remains steady, as long as the home video market in the United States keeps expanding (he seems to do reasonably well within it), there is no reason why he cannot continue to make movies at the pace he prefers. Whether that is the best possible strategy for him will doubtless remain a subject for debate among his supporters.

The debate ignores what we might call the Brass Balls factor. Diane Keaton put it this way to John Lahr: "He has great balls. . . . He's got balls to the floor." By which she means that he is the exact opposite of his screen character. He is a willful man, a man who will do what he feels he has to do, say what he thinks needs to be said, no matter the obstacles.

For the reasons we've already mentioned, he needs to make a movie every year. Therefore he will make a movie every year. He needs to take up in those films whatever topic is pressing upon him. Therefore he will forge a film that speaks to and of that need. The same is true of his private life. "The heart wants what it wants," he famously said at the time his relationship with Soon-Yi Previn became public knowledge. And he followed his heart, knowing full well that contumely would also follow.

Has this caused him permanent damage? It is hard to say. I do not think anyone believes the hysterical (and preposterous) charges of child abuse Mia Farrow brought against him; certainly the courts did not. But one observes, particularly among women of an age and class that he could once have counted among his supporters, a reluctance to embrace his work since the scandal. They see his relationship with Soon-Yi as virtually incestuous.

To me this is an absurdity. Soon-Yi is Korean by birth, an orphan adopted by Farrow and her onetime husband, André Previn. She was related to no one in her adoptive mother's household by blood—certainly not to Woody, whose relationship with Mia Farrow, to whom he was not married, had by the early 1990s become a professional and companionate one: they made movies together; they were seen together on public occasions; they often dined together in restaurants.

And Woody continued to visit Farrow's apartment almost daily in order to see their child, Satchel, who was born to him and Farrow when their relationship had been an intimate one. Twelve other children were living in her apartment, but with the exception of two—a girl named Dylan and a boy named Moses, both of whom he legally adopted—Woody was not close with any of them. They were Farrow's responsibility, which she exercised, according to Woody, in a helter-skelter sort of way.

Soon-Yi had become part of the Farrow ménage two years before Farrow and Woody met, and it was not until she was legally of age, a college student, that he began noticing her— as an attractive, intelligent young woman. There was no bar—legal or, in my opinion, moral—to his making his interest known to her.

She was, of course, several decades younger than Woody when they embarked on their affair, a circumstance that never sets well with moralizing America—though it seems to accept, with no more than the occasionally raised eyebrow, the fact that many rich and famous men acquire second "trophy" wives who are much younger than they are. In any event, Soon-Yi was free to make any romantic decision she wished. Whether, once the storm broke about them, both she and Woody might have wished that their eyes had not met across a crowded room, we cannot know. But so they did.

And so what? Their affair was not—shall we put it mildly?—in perfect "taste." It affronted middle-class morality. It reminded us of the discomfiting assaults on romantic convention that had so often been Woody's subjects in his films. Perhaps people might have said, "If you can imagine a transgression, you are capable of it."

But they didn't. As for Woody and Soon-Yi, they were housebound for days, weeks, unable to venture out because the paparazzi were permanently staked out around Woody's apartment house. He was, as well, engulfed in the legal nightmare resulting from Farrow's charges of child abuse. These were entirely unsubstantiated, but Woody was unable to see Satchel unencumbered by a social worker, and later his visitation rights were severely circumscribed. Of late he has not seen him or his adopted kids at all. It was as bad a nightmare as any public figure has ever endured.

There are only two possible responses to such an ordeal. One is to go completely to ground, to become the recluse that elements of the press had always implied Woody was. The other is simply to go on with your life.

Perhaps we need to digress for a moment on the subject of reclusiveness. The press that dominated the coverage of this "scandal" was the tabloid press, both print and TV. They had always been mystified by Woody, because he refused to play by their primitive rules.

These are quite simple. When you are caught in their lights, you smile for them. They know they're pests, but if you make a little implied joke out of their intrusiveness they will actually share it with you and minimize their demands. It helps, too, to grant them a few dopey interviews on, say, the occasion of your latest movie. By thus acknowledging their (self) importance, you disarm them.

This is the way the movie game (and the celebrity game) is played in America. If you don't play it that way, the press senses contempt—not just for itself but for its slack-jawed readers and viewers. They remember that, in Woody's case, when he was nominated for the Academy Awards he did not even bother to show up for the ceremonies. How strange is that? But, Oscars or not, they begin to paint you as a weirdo. They imagine things about your life that are simply, often ludicrously, untrue.

But Woody never had any need of that crowd. Readers of, say, the *New York Post* are not, by and large, people who are ever likely to see his movies. So why bother with it or with them? That Woody has always made himself available to the serious press, granting it thoughtful, extensive—even book-length—interviews, cuts no ice with them. It is to them the equivalent of his contentment with making movies for a minority audience—almost un-American.

Eventually every public figure does something to offend the public. And Woody's offense was no mere messy divorce or minor drug bust. It could be played as a dark psychodrama. It became, whether the media was conscious of what it was doing or not, an occasion for revenge.

One could easily have excused Woody if he had fled the country. But he did not. He did not even try to escape the city. He had not, in his estimation, done anything wrong. So when the photographers decamped his front door, he went back to his usual routines. He played with his jazz band on Monday nights, as he had for decades. He went to the Knicks games when he felt like it. He perhaps wandered the streets a little less frequently than before, but he went to the movies, he went out to dinner, and, above all, he continued to make his movies on precisely the schedule he always had. He assumed—correctly—that the ever-distractible media would soon turn its attention elsewhere.

He was right in his behavior and right about the media wandering off. The pattern of his life has been preserved. In some ways, it seems to me, it has been enhanced. His courage—the brassiness of his balls, if you will—had been tested, and he had not been found wanting. Moreover he emerged with something he had not enjoyed before—a happy marriage. Soon-Yi is a very intelligent, attentive, and forthright woman; in the exchanges with Woody that I have witnessed, one senses a serious and well-balanced relationship in which, clearly, she is not the least bit dominated by his fame, accomplishments, or brains. They listen to each other sympathetically, and when they disagree it is rather obviously within the parameters of a sympathetic affection.

I do not think Woody has escaped entirely unscathed from this ordeal. The domestic audience for his films has demonstrably dwindled from its never exactly robust highs. That's probably not entirely attributable to the "scandal," yet it surely took some toll.

But, as we've seen, his audience has been drifting away for

a long time. Comedy in America is now either crass and aimed at an essentially juvenile audience, or it is weary and strained in the way that romantic comedy aimed at an older crowd—*You've Got Mail, Maid in Manhattan, Two Weeks Notice*—has been for many years. If one sees a comedy that is seriously funny about, say, domestic disturbances, it is likely to be French. Certainly it will have subtitles.

Indeed, looked at purely as economic phenomena, Woody Allen films perform pretty much the way foreign films now do in the United States. They tend to play in limited runs in a relatively small number of theaters, their audience is not at all a mainstream crowd, and their grosses are counted in a range well under $10 million, which is about what a failed major studio release takes in on its opening weekend.

To put the matter simply, Woody Allen is now, as far as the United States of America is concerned, an almost fully marginalized filmmaker. His career now looks like one of those from the great age of international filmmaking, extending from the late fifties through the seventies. It is a career— all his protestations to the contrary—like Bergman's or Fellini's or Kurosawa's or Truffaut's (to name just a few of that era's ornaments), that belongs now to the cineastes and cinephiles of the world, not to the mass audience.

There appeared in the *New York Times* in June 2002 a very curious front-page article. In it the reporter contrasted Woody's appearance in the courtroom—for his suit against Jean Doumanian's company, in which he charged that he had been cheated out of substantial sums by accounting procedures—and the audience at an afternoon performance of *Hollywood Ending.* In court Woody was sticking to his guns, but his testimony surely lacked something in legalistic precision. It seemed—or could be made to seem—shambling, out of it. Meanwhile, at the theater, only four or five people were watching his movie. There were far more people in court. The implication was clear: Woody had become irrelevant, both as a man and as a filmmaker.

It was, in many ways, a shameful article, a slightly pathetic attempt by the greatest of American newspapers—and a newspaper that over the years had supported Woody with critical encomiums and admiring profiles—to appear hip, on the contemptuous cutting edge. For one thing, Woody's court action was far from frivolous, and I am given to understand (not by him) that the settlement he reached with Doumanian favored him. For another, this was very late in *Hollywood Ending*'s run and on a midweek afternoon at that. Other pictures released at the same time, and far more generally successful, were surely doing similar business at that moment.

In short, the piece was motivelessly malign, yet another attempt by the mainstream press—it is a habit it has lately fallen into—to align itself with the populist press without dirtying its skirts. We're just reporting, folks—but in such a way as to confirm a fall from grace in a respectable journal.

Reading that article I began to wonder if we should think of Woody as a filmmaker at all. I wondered if we should instead think of him as a novelist who happens to "write" on film. Like the purveyors of what we have come to call "literary fiction," he has a small, loyal audience. Like them, he has a small number of themes to which he returns more or less obsessively with varying results, but almost never without admirable ambition. Like them, he is made nervous by the attention of the mass media (think Jonathan Franzen and his famous unease with Oprah and her book club). Like them, his work is primarily moved by his own needs, not the audience's expectations. Like them, he is an isolated figure in a mass culture almost entirely moved by momentary sensation and interested primarily in grosses, ratings, big deals, celebrity preening, and (temporary, generally curable) celebrity folly.

It requires—well, yes—balls to the floor to persist in a life dedicated to your own vision, your own obsessions, in a culture of that kind. People will hypocritically mourn your passage into "irrelevancy."

I clearly do not think that is true of Woody. Looking back on his career to date, I believe that, without him or anyone else quite knowing it, he was an early test case of a major shift in the way popular culture regards people who define themselves in terms other than last weekend's grosses and celebrity showboating. I also think—despite Woody's dubiety about the workings of posterity—that a small but passionate group will continue to attend his work and take it seriously. There is already a large body of book-length critical work about his films; there are perhaps more such tomes about him than about any other living American filmmaker. More will follow as the body of his work becomes the more or less exclusive property of the intellectual and academic classes. There will be retrospectives too, and they will not be unlike the one he skewered in *Stardust Memories*. Academic conferences will also follow, and they will not be indifferent to the fact that Woody made his assertions in a shifting American climate which became, over the course of his career, inimical not merely to Woody's themes but to his manner of working, his very attitudes toward that revised (and cheapened) cultural climate.

Some years ago Woody and I fell to talking about Ingmar Bergman, and he said, "It's almost irrelevant to say you like this one better than that one, to say I like *The Seventh Seal* better than I like *Shame*. They are all aspects of him." I have no wish to embarrass Woody by invoking the name of his beloved master. I do hope, however, that this essay encourages readers to look at the entire body of his work in a way they mostly have not. I hope they may set aside their gossip and speculation about the man, set aside their "likes" and "dislikes," and begin to see his work as a coherent statement about themes of some importance to all of us. I hope, as well, they will see that his work represents aspects of an aspiring, various, and serious artist who has refracted back to us aspects of our times, our lives, our immortally quavering souls, in ways that I suspect will remain instructive (and, yes, hugely amusing) for a long time to come.

No, I'm not talking about "the artist's Catholicism." But I am talking about—have been talking about—some films that will, whether Woody believes it or not, outlive him at least for a time, outlive a lot of movies that made more money, generated more "buzz" than his usually have. This is not everything. But it is not nothing either.

The Interview

It seems to me that as a young guy you were unlike a lot of cineastes in that you showed no precocious interest in being a film-maker. Or am I wrong about that?

I was interested when I started in being a playwright. I had no particular interest in films. In those days, when I was a teenager, movies were silly and plays had all the heavyweight cachet in the United States. The playwrights were the guys who were doing good work, and the filmmakers were basically studio people who were for the most part turning out, you know, commercial product, so I wasn't really too interested in being a filmmaker.

I only became interested in film after I wrote the script to *What's New, Pussycat?* As a writer, it was obligatory for me to stick around the set and watch. And this was the quintessential Hollywood production—almost a satire on itself—with everything loathsome that won laughs (or cringes) associated with that kind of film. I couldn't bear the picture when it came out. I was completely embarrassed and humiliated by the experience. I vowed that I would never write another film script unless I could direct it. And that's how I got into films.

But I was certainly never anyone who had a camera when

I was younger. To this day, you know, I couldn't care less about the technology of it. All the technological advances made in film, as far as I'm concerned, are only valuable in so far as they enable you to tell a story effectively. But there are many films that come out in which people are so smitten with the technology that it becomes the content of the film, and the end in itself. I get put off by it, I have no interest in it.

On another level though, you have said more than once that as a kid you loved going to movies, that they had an important function for you as a kind of escape.

I grew up on movies. I lived in Brooklyn, which was, you know, about forty-five minutes away from Manhattan by train. What was accessible to me in my early years was not the theater, it was films. There was no television in those days, and so I adored film when I was a kid and used to go—I'm talking, you know from when I was, let's say, five years old, six, seven, eight, nine, ten, those years—to movies constantly, just constantly.

In those days the parents used to admonish the kids for not getting enough sunshine, before they realized that it gave you cancer, and they would get angry if the kids were going to the movies and not going out and lying on the beach and, and sucking in the sun. But I used to go to the movies whenever I could, and it was possible for me very often—four, five times a week. Because in my neighborhood in Brooklyn in those days there were fifty movie theaters virtually within walking distance of [my] house.

I mean, I would walk for ten minutes and would hit fifteen movie theaters with different double features in them. And movies were twenty cents to get in, at my age, at that time, and some movies were even less. I can remember going to the movies for twelve cents, and getting, uh, a little gift of a gun that made a noise, or a pinwheel or a comic book, and seeing short subjects. This was all for no money at all.

And when I got a tiny bit older, I recall when Friday would come and we'd get out of school at three o'clock, I used to race in a dead run from school to get to the cinema before it became too late. They wouldn't let [unaccompanied] children in after a certain time because we would start to encroach on the evening performances. And I would sometimes make it, sometimes not make it. If I didn't make it I'd have to go find a stranger to take me into the movies and, and pose as his child or her child. And so I saw everything that came out, and loved it.

And then when I was a middle teenager, after the war, there was a huge influx of European cinema in the United States, and that was a turning point in my life, because suddenly I saw that movies could actually be something substantially wonderful. [They] didn't have to be these vacuous cowboy pictures and shoot-'em-up pictures and dopey little comedies that weren't really very funny and innocuous love stories that were escapist, but were not really escapist because they weren't good enough.

We only got the best of their films over here, and I really did develop a taste for movies at that point, but still I [would have been] very content to have a life in the theater and was looking forward to being a playwright [because] this kind of, uh, adult cinema, or serious cinema, didn't exist [in America]. The people that were writing for the theater at the time were, you know, Tennessee Williams and Arthur Miller, and William Inge, and, and you could really do something substantial in the theater. [Had I been] a European I might have diverted from a love of theater earlier to a love of film, because the potential for doing some interesting things was there.

But yet in a number of your movies you've paid really warm sweet tribute to those trivial American movies. I think of Purple Rose of Cairo. *I think of* Husbands and Wives *where they go to see* Double Indemnity *and they love it. There's a nice tribute to Orson Welles's* Lady from Shanghai *with the mirrors breaking in* Manhattan Murder Mystery. *Obviously you have an affection for those movies, or maybe an affection for their part in your own past.*

I do have an affection for those early films, for the early kind of trivial films, because we all have an affection for the things that we grow up on, like the popular music of the time or the films or the radio programs. It's really linked more to nostalgia. But it's not based on the merits of the pictures. When I could see most of them for what they were, I didn't have a great deal of respect for them, [though] I did [retain] an affectionate feeling for them. [But] when I've utilized them in, in later movies, I've utilized the few that I thought were superb by any standards, like *Double Indemnity* or the work of Orson Welles. But I would not think of *Purple Rose of Cairo* in any way as an affectionate homage to that kind of film. I would think of that as a dark film about a woman who was forced to choose between fantasy and reality and naturally had to choose reality, because if you choose fantasy, that way lies madness, and so she chose reality, and as it does in real life it crushes her at the end.

I didn't mean to skip so far ahead to Purple Rose, *but to me one of its salient points is that the Jeff Daniels character has left these people on the screen bereft. Without him their picture is stuck. And one of them rather poignantly says, in effect, "Well, I liked it the way it was because we always knew what we were doing." In other words, they play the same movie endlessly, always in exactly the same way. Is that movie partly about certainty, and the fact that if you pull certainty out of the equation people get very tense and nervous? Is that a fair reading of an aspect of that movie?*

Well, reality has no certainty to it. Fantasy has got certainty, and fantasy is much better than reality. I mean unfortunately we can't live in fantasy, and we're forced to live in this grim reality that we find ourselves in for inexplicable reasons. But one of the many, many appeals of fantasy is that it has got a calming regularity to it, and when you look at, let's say, these fantasy movies that Fred Astaire was in, or the sophisticated comedies—the viewer could go to the cinema, put down his fifty cents or whatever it cost him to go, his twenty-five cents, and know that he was seeing these familiar faces that he'd seen in other films, and they were playing the same thing again, they were doing what they were supposed to do.

[In that way] film is more mythological than dramatic. I always knew when I was a kid, if I went to the movies, that John Wayne was going to play a certain thing, and Humphrey Bogart would play a certain thing, and James Cagney and Gary Cooper and Bob Hope. And as long as they played that thing I was happy. It was really the same myth being reenacted over and over and over again, much as one would read a Greek myth or a Norse myth, and see the little anecdote being reenacted countless times by the same gods, whose attributes one could predict.

And so if I had gone to a movie—this never happened—and seen Bob Hope suddenly in a dramatic role, I would have felt very put off by it. I mean, when I was much older it would have been explainable to me, and I would have taken it for what it was but wish that it didn't happen too often. But when I was younger and went to a movie there was a kind of regularity to the whole equation of fantasy, and certainly in cinema that's calming and reassuring, and in the end I wish it were the pervasive mode of existence. But it's not.

So is that in essence what Purple Rose of Cairo *is about, that desire for the predictability of fantasy and the way it can transport you? And then the crushing disappointment when the fantasy is taken away?*

Purple Rose is about this woman whose life is bleak and grim and seeks all this escapism in the cinema, where she gets it, you know, in the way they used to dish it out in the 1930s. I mean she just gets all the escape she can hope for in these romantic situations where people live in penthouses with white telephones and go to these wonderful nightclubs and drink champagne and are never at a loss for a *bon mot* or a, a great quip, and their romances turn out wonderfully. But she is forced to choose at some point in her life between existing in that fantasy and existing in real life, and some instinct in her tells her that she's got to exist in the real world, because to exist in the fantasy world is psychosis. And by choosing the real world, which we all must do, she is inevitably crushed by it, as we all inevitably are.

So you see that movie as—maybe tragic is too big a word for it, but—as a serious movie? A movie with tragic overtones? I don't know how to put it.

Well, when I was writing *Purple Rose,* I only had half the movie. I thought, what a funny idea—the guy steps off the screen and into this woman's life. But I put it aside for six months, 'cause I had no real story.

And it was only when the idea occurred to me—and I guess it's a tragic idea rather than a pathetic idea—the actor playing that part comes, and she's forced to choose between the screen image and the real-life person, and she picks the real-life person, and it kills her, not kills her, but it just hurts her very badly. That's when I knew I had a movie. And when they showed this movie out of town, in Boston, United Artists, or Orion, I can't remember who I made it for—showed it, and they called me up and they said, "We love this movie."

And they said to me on the phone, "You know, if you had a happy ending on this movie we really think we could go through the roof with it. It would be a great commercial movie." And I said, that's the movie, and the only reason I made the movie is because of the tragic ending, otherwise I wouldn't have even made the film. And they said, yeah, we figured you were going to say that, and as usual they were very supportive and very nice. But for me the, the tragic end of that movie was the only reason I did the picture.

You mentioned earlier a long list of people that were mythic on the screen, like Bob Hope. And I know that you did the Lincoln Center tribute to him. He obviously had more influence on you than John Wayne. There was some part of you, wasn't there, that really wanted to emulate him as a comic screen figure?

To me, probably, Bob Hope was the biggest comic influence on my performing. I always adored him when I was younger, and it's an adoration that's never left me to this day. This morning I was watching *Fancy Pants* on television. If I'm surfing through the TV channels and I hit a Bob Hope movie—I don't mean one of the later ones, where he was way over the hill and they're not very good—but one of the prime-year Bob Hope movies, let's say, forties and fifties—I can never turn them off, as many times as I've seen them. And I always laugh. I mean I was laughing out loud, by myself, on my treadmill, watching Bob Hope. The movies are not cine-matic masterpieces, but he's so great, and I felt he never got sufficient credit for it. People don't appreciate him, because the movies were not artistic movies, or there wasn't a strain of tragedy in his work, or something. But he's so gifted as a comic persona. And there were times. . . .

The other great deliverer of lines, of course, has always been Groucho Marx. And Groucho was clearly a genius, and everyone who writes about film and who knows the history of film would agree that there was something genius about the Marx Brothers. They didn't have a tragic strain to their com-edy—they had a surrealistic strain. But there was an element of genius that's very apparent there.

Hope has every bit of Groucho's strength as a deliverer of lines—he's every bit as great as Groucho—but he's more real. Groucho was a clown, and you can never picture Groucho in any kind of a realistic situation. It's always surrealistic—the painted-on moustache—and he's clearly something that's stepped out of unreality into the real world. Hope gets away with these lines and behavior in a real context—he can play a real person, a love interest, a guy posing as a private detective, uh, someone posing as a swordsman, and his work is wonder-ful.

Dick Cavett once said, "Try doing some of those lines yourself, and you see what a touch he has. You appreciate what a touch he has." It's soufflé light and it's so brilliant. You've got to listen for the lyrics, but they're there. And of course when I proselytize and, and, and grab people around the lapels, you know, like the ancient mariner, they look at some of the movies, and some of the movies are not so great.

So I have to show them the sections that are great. And you can extrapolate that with someone like Jerry Lewis as well. You know, there are clear-cut moments that if you can get rid of the other things that block your vision of it, you really can see what an enormous talent the person is. They may have not been in a good movie, or they [are] maybe being too crazy in the rest of the movie, or whatever objection you may validly have about the film, [but] these guys were tremendous natural talents, and when used properly, enormously effective. And for me Hope was the, the king of them.

Your own early screen persona, maybe like the figure in Bananas *or even the character in* Take the Money and Run, *owes something to Bob Hope. In other words, like Bob Hope he's kind of cowardly, but he's also kind of a wolf, as we used to say, with women. He's not necessarily a victim, though he is victimized frequently enough.*

I think that I do Bob Hope all the time, I'm just nowhere near as good. But I do him all the time. If you look at a picture like *Love and Death*—when I put together film clips for the Lincoln Center tribute to Bob Hope I included some clips from *Love and Death* to, to parallel them with Bob Hope, to show what an influence he was on me. I mean it's, it's just shameless how I steal from him—I don't mean steal the content of jokes, but I do him.

If I'm watching him with a friend of mine, if I watch a

Bob Hope movie with Diane Keaton, she just sees it. You can't miss it. What people don't see is that I'm not as good. He's the genuine article. He's Bob Hope, and I'm . . . you know, it's the anxiety of influence. I'm trying to lean on him and yet anxious about it, but he's all over my work in a shameless way.

I'm interested in the remark you made about Love and Death. *Can you name a couple of the things that you did in there where you were particularly shamelessly hooking from Bob?*

Oh, all over the place. Uh, now I haven't seen this picture in God knows how long, twenty years or whenever I made it, but there's this party and I get introduced to a very attractive woman and I'm posing as a hero, which is something he did in all his movies, and I'm really not a hero, but I'm pretending to be a hero. And she invites me to her bedroom at night. And I come to her bedroom and I'm tossing off the one-liners, the same one-liners you could write for him, which I did effectively enough to set my table, as Willy Loman would say, but not the way he would. You know, he would do them better. But I did them as best I could.

We had a conversation twenty years ago, and you talked about coming up out of the subway and seeing the world of Manhattan for the first time. Tell me about that and what that meant to you, that sense of emergence you felt as a kid.

The first time I came into Manhattan that I can recall was an astonishing experience, [even though] I lived [only] forty-five minutes away. But, you know, when you're four years old, five years old, you don't travel freely. And my father took me and we got off the train from Avenue J in Brooklyn in Times Square in Manhattan. And when you came upstairs it was the most astonishing thing that one could ever imagine. As far as the eye could see there were movie houses in every direction. Now I thought there were a lot, and there were, where I grew up in Brooklyn, but here, every twenty-five feet or every thirty feet, there were movie houses—up and down Forty-second Street, up and down Broadway, and it appeared to me the most glamorous kind of thing.

It was the configuration of all the signs, the Howard Clothes sign and the Camel sign, all those things that have become icons now. And there were the streets mobbed with soldiers and sailors, and they all looked great in their uniforms. And the women, at that time, had the Betty Grable, Rita Hayworth, Veronica Lake look—that's what they were all aspiring toward. And they'd be walking around the streets and they'd be holding hands with sailors, and there would be guys up against the building selling apparently stringless dancing dolls, you know, and, and papaya stands and shooting galleries.

I mean it was not terribly unlike where Fred Astaire is walking in *The Band Wagon* at the beginning. That was not exaggerated. It was a built variation of it. It was an astonishing thing to see.

And the minute I saw that, you know, all that I ever wanted to do was live in Manhattan and work in Manhattan. I mean, I couldn't get enough of it. At every conceivable moment from then on, when I could con my parents into taking me into Manhattan, I did it. And when I was quite young—in those days you didn't have to worry about getting slaughtered on the subway—when I was in the fifth grade, or fourth grade, the fare was only a nickel, and my friend and I would get together a half-dollar or a dollar maybe, if we were lucky, and we would, on a Saturday morning, get dressed up and go into Manhattan.

Here were two little kids and we'd walk around, and we would go eat at the Automat, and look in the windows at Jack Dempsey's, and look at the photographs in Lindy's window. And it was just, you know, everything I've tried to communicate to people for years in my films. And that was just the Broadway area. As I spent more and more time in the city I saw what Greenwich Village was like, and I saw what Fifth Avenue was like, and the Upper East Side, and Gramercy Park. . . .

And to this day I feel the same way about it. I've been all over the world—I've been to every major city in the world—and I love some of them. I mean I really love some of them. But there's nothing like Manhattan, just nothing like it. It remains, you know, the most enchanting and spectacular city on the face of the earth.

Would you say that Radio Days *is your biggest tribute to that Manhattan of your yearning childhood?*

Radio Days was a film [where] I was able to show a certain amount of my childhood comprehension of Manhattan. Most of it took place out in Rockaway where the family lived, but there were a couple of scenes where we came into Manhattan, and a couple of scenes that took place amongst the radio personalities, and for the money I had to make the picture that's the best I could show it.

And, Santo did an incredible job, Santo Loquasto my scenic designer, did an unbelievable job of re-creating Broadway and those signs in the studio. It was a very tough thing to do. And we went around and scouted locations and found that Macy's was relatively unchanged, and there was one last Automat on Forty-second Street and Lexington or Third Ave— Third Avenue, I think. . . .

They took me, as a kid, in the movie to this place that had an exhibition of war things, I remembered it from my childhood. It was in the Radio City building. It was an, uh, an exhibit that my father took me to when my mother was in the hospital with my sister giving birth. And we visited her and, and then he took me into the city and took me to this exhibition of, you know, guns and walkie-talkies and canteens and all army stuff that was colorful for a kid to look at—binoculars and things. And in the course of my adult life I met one other adult who remembered that and knew where it was in the city.

The whole sequence where they take this little kid to Radio City Music Hall, and the vaulting glamour of that place, overwhelms him—did you have any specific experience like that? Or is it a fantasy projection?

No, I have specific memories of being taken when I was younger to a few places. One was the Radio City Music Hall to see *Madame Curie,* and being just overwhelmed—you couldn't believe the experience unless you went through it. And when we went back to shoot at the Radio City Music Hall, and went into the bathrooms there—I mean the bathrooms were more stylish and beautiful than people's homes now. I mean they were just these gorgeous, deco bathrooms, large and beautiful, as though they were done by the best scenic designer in Hollywood.

And also the Paramount. The Paramount, which no longer exists, was amazing. And I'll never forget playing hooky from school, and going into Manhattan, [where] you could go to the movies, which you couldn't do in Brooklyn, at ten o'clock in the morning. And going into the Paramount Theater at ten o'clock in the morning, knowing I didn't have to go to school, and seeing a movie, and then when the movie was over, rising out of the pit would be Duke Ellington and you'd hear "Take the A Train" filling that theater. You know, it would take the top of your head off.

And then comedians would come out and these poor guys, they're working at eleven o'clock in the morning, or something, to a tenth of a house, on a rainy Wednesday morning. But it was so thrilling to, to see those things. And I remember any number of New York experiences—certainly the first time I ever went to Lindy's in my life. I, I just couldn't believe it. And the first time that I ever took a walk on Fifth Avenue was amazing. They had those, those green, double-decker buses and, you know, the city was astonishing.

I took many walks in the course of my life with my father in Manhattan, and he had a very good memory (he was born in 1900) of which places were speakeasies and which places were gambling places, and who was murdered where, and what happened. I used to walk on Fifth Avenue with him and in the West Forties, and he showed me all the spots in the city. And it was just great.

I remember when I used to go on dates when I was a teenager, I would take these innocent little girls into the city, and I knew the city well and, and they were put off by it, you know. It was too much for them. I would go to this little place and that little place to get a drink, and they didn't want to know from that. They were teenage girls who couldn't care less about it. . . .

Well, as a young writer you became a little bit a part of that world. In other words, you were selling gag lines to columnists and you were starting to be a gag writer on television, which isn't quite the world you came to inhabit, but I'm sure it had a kind of raffish glamour for you. Or did it?

When I was an early teenager I thought about writing a little bit. But, you know, the guys that I liked were serious writers, for the most part—Faulkner and Hemingway and, as I say, Tennessee Williams. And then as I got to later high school my friends were all making life decisions. They were going to go to college or pre-med school or becoming lawyers, and I didn't know what it was that I wanted to do.

And I, just for a lark, was writing around a little bit and wrote some jokes, and I was instantly successful with them. Someone said, why don't you send these in, 'cause they print these in the newspapers sometimes—you know, just for fun. So I just put them in a little envelope and threw it in the mailbox, and I suddenly found that my name appeared in the newspapers with a joke. And it was an astonishing touch of fame, you know, 'cause I had no connection to the outside world whatsoever—I was this jerky little kid in high school and suddenly my name appeared.

And, you know, I took great pains to sign a different name, 'cause I thought God, if anyone ever used this it would be so embarrassing to have my name printed in the newspaper. So I changed my name to Woody Allen and suddenly a few weeks later they printed another one and another one, and after two months, three months, I got a phone call at home—my father was driving a cab, my mother was working at a flower store—[from a publicity firm]. And they said we called the newspapers and asked who this guy is, 'cause we like these jokes, and would you be interested in a job?

And I said, you know, I go to high school, so I don't get out of school until one o'clock, and I can't get into Manhattan till two o'clock. And they said that's okay. You can come here and, and you can write some jokes for us. And what I'd do is, I would write the jokes, and they would attribute those jokes to personalities and they would get in the columns, like Walter Winchell's column and Earl Wilson's column, they would thereby get publicity for the clients they had.

And so I would get out of school at, at one o'clock, and I'd go over to the subway and get on, and start writing jokes. And for me, you know, I've often said this, if you can do it, there's nothing to it. You know, it's like drawing. I can't draw, so I'm astonished at a kid sitting next to me in class who will draw a rabbit or something, I'm amazed by it. For him it's nothing, and he wonders why I can't do it. Or the kid next to me has got an ear for music and can sing on pitch perfectly.

Well, I could write jokes, so there was nothing to it. So I got on the subway and started writing them, and I would write fifty jokes a day, easily. I would have twenty, twenty-five done by the time I got into Manhattan, and then sit down to the typewriter and, and write another twenty, twenty-five. It was not hard. These were not Oscar Wilde or something. They were, you know, mother-in-law jokes, parking-space jokes, political jokes, topical jokes.

I was working there for a short while and their clients were getting their names in the paper and, and then I got a phone call asking me if I would be interested in writing on a radio show. And I did write on the radio show. Sure, I was very interested. And then I got an offer to write on, what in those days was called a "simulcast." It was radio and television at the same time. And I said yes, and I suddenly found that I was working and I was so naive about it. I was writing the Herb Shriner show. He was a comedian at that time and had a very popular television show, and I was one of the writers on the show.

And the first week I had written a show, and I went in—it was live on Saturday night—and I got on the back of the line of the studio audience to go in. And I was waiting—you know, there were three hundred people ahead of me—and Herb's manager came walking by and said, "Why are you waiting in line?"

And I said, "Well, you know, I want to see the show. I wrote, you know, the jokes." And he said, "You don't have to wait in line," and he took me back through the stage entrance. It was the first time that ever happened to me. And I was backstage watching it and, of course, this whole world was amazing to me, you know, 'cause, I was just a kid. I didn't know what was going on. I was seventeen years old, and I was earning more money than my parents put together had ever earned in their life.

And from there I got a job as a staff writer at NBC. They wanted to develop new writers. And they had a big program and they hired me for a very substantial salary, for me at that time I mean. . . . The kids in my neighborhood were earning I don't know what—the minimum wage was like fifty-five cents an hour or something, and I was earning like sixteen hundred dollars a week. And then, then I got to write on other television shows, and was earning very high salaries.

And I always thought to myself, well, television will be a good stepping-stone. I'll learn how to write eventually, and I'll develop my craft, and then I'll write for the theater. I had no interest in the movies whatsoever, except, you know, to go to the movies and, and be entertained, but that's how I started. I had no interest in being a performer. I mean, the thought of being a performer would have been crazy to me. It wouldn't have occurred to me.

That's interesting to me. For example, your very first movie— well, the first real Woody Allen movie, Take the Money and Run—*takes the form of a television documentary, doesn't it? It's this sort of sententious voice talking about this dreadful criminal. But it's like a television program. It draws from a television form that was familiar at that time.*

Take the Money and Run was a pseudo-documentary. The idea of doing a documentary, which I later finally perfected when I did *Zelig,* was with me from the first day I started movies. I thought that was an ideal vehicle for doing comedy, because the documentary format was very serious, so you were immediately operating in an area where any little thing you did upset the seriousness and was thereby funny. And you could tell your story laugh by laugh by laugh. I wrote that with Mickey Rose, a friend of mine from high school, and the object of the movie was for every inch of it to be a laugh.

We didn't care about anything else except that each pro- gression of the story, every inch of the way, was a laugh. And the documentary format was ideal for that.

What about Bananas? *You've got the Howard Cosell charac-*
ter who's always intruding on the death of the dictator or the love
bout at the end of the film. Again, there's a television component to
Bananas.

Well, *Bananas* did have that one scene in it, the opening
scene of Howard Cosell giving a firsthand report on an assassination, treating an assassination in a South American country like it was a sporting event. But that was just, I think,
coincidence. That was the only television reference in that
picture. And that was just, I thought, a good joke. Latin
American politics was so unstable for so many years, and there
was so much violence down there, that the thought of a traditional assassination that was covered by television much the
same way you'd cover the, the Olympics, or whatever, seemed
a funny joke to me.

And of course Howard added that documentary touch of
reality to it that made it work. It might not have worked in
somebody else's hands, but he brought to it just a . . .

Did you have something more in mind in Bananas *than a*
string of gags? Was there more of an overarching idea there than in
Take the Money and Run?

Bananas also was basically just a stream of gags hung on a
very thin plot line. What people don't realize is that pictures
like *Bananas* are very, very structured. They can't see the
structure, so they think that structure set in for me with *Annie*
Hall years later. But *Bananas* is very structured. There's the as-

sassination at the beginning, and then we pick up the life of the lead character, and we go along with that life. And then he goes away to South America to forget his unhappy romance, and all of that, which had been very well set up at the beginning, comes to bear fruit later. I mean it was well structured. But the structure really becomes an armature on which to hang a million crazy jokes, which is what the film is basically about. But to think that it is just jokes is wrong. But [still], what we wanted to do is make people laugh as hard as we could, as hard as they could, and we went for every comic bit we could think of. . . .

You said before that you thought structure came only with Annie Hall. *But it strikes me that both* Sleeper *and* Love and Death *do seem more structured. It seems there's a real central idea to them that's moving them, in a more obvious way than in, say,* Bananas *or* Take the Money and Run.

When I said *Annie Hall* before, it may be I'm forgetting and I should have said *Sleeper.* That was clearly a picture that wasn't just gags but had a story to it. And *Love and Death* also had a structure.

It's just that people used to think that pictures like *Take the Money and Run* and *Bananas,* because of the wildness in the humor, were unstructured. But they weren't. The jokes were surreal and crazy—they were cartoons, just as *Love and Death* is a cartoon. But *Sleeper* [had] a more obvious structure to it. And the reason that the structure's more apparent is because it had less gags.

The gags didn't violate the reality of the story, whereas in *Take the Money and Run* or *Bananas* or *Love and Death,* the jokes violated anything we wanted. Nothing was sacred— they could be anachronistic, they could be surrealistic, it didn't matter. You know, *Sleeper* was a very ambitious project for me, which I failed in. I came to United Artists [with] this idea to do a three-hour picture, with an intermission.

The first hour and a half would be a picture of me as a character in Manhattan, going through his life and his love life and whatever story I could get out of that, and at the end of the hour and a half I fall into this cryogenic vat. And the second half of the picture, when the curtain opens, or when we fade in, it's two hundred years later, and suddenly everything looks completely different. And this was a good idea. I just didn't have the stamina to write so much. I didn't have the will to carry it off.

I wasn't good enough to, to work for months on the first movie, and then when that was finished put it aside and work for months on the future part. I just didn't have it in me to do it. But it was a nice idea.

The other point you said you wanted to make about Sleeper *was . . . ?*

At that point in my, my life, I was for whatever ridiculous reason very taken with the films of Chaplin and Keaton in relation to myself. Not ridiculous that I be taken with their films, they're great, but I was trying to learn from them, and I had the idea that it was easier working in a silent era. Most people think that silent comedies were harder, 'cause you didn't have a voice, you couldn't speak. But silent films were easier. When you added the voice it became much more complicated; it's really the difference between checkers and chess. Consequently both Chaplin and Keaton were killed when the voices were added—it becomes much less abstract and much more real. And so I thought when I made *Sleeper,* being so interested in Keaton and Chaplin at the time, that I would wake up in the future, and in the future no one was allowed to speak—with the tyranny maybe the guys in some office someplace high up and out of reach could talk if they wanted, but the population was not allowed to speak.

And so I could do a silent film, with a very good motivation [for silence] and could do all those silent gags. But that was, again, a nice idea that drifted by the wayside as just not productive enough for me to pursue—and perhaps a good thing that I didn't, because in retrospect who wants to see me doing those pratfalls and balletic things that I'm probably incapable of doing.

To me the funniest sequence in it is when your character is pretending to be a robot and they're going to take his head off, which is basically a silent sequence.

It's silent, yeah—it was intended in its most original form to be a silent situation, and I got some of that in when I played the robot in it, where I couldn't speak and just had to do things. But if I had done the idea purely it would have been an hour and a half in Manhattan, normal, and then (*snaps fingers*), I'd fall into a cryogenic vat, wake up in the future, all white and strange looking, two hundred years later. But laziness . . .

I would have missed all those jokes about "Now they've discovered cigarettes are good for you," and . . .

Right, you would have missed . . .

Those are very funny.

You would have missed the verbal, the verbal humor for, for what that's worth. Sure. And I'm probably better at delivering that than, than I would be, you know, falling off a ladder or something.

When did you get interested in Chaplin? Does that go back to childhood?

Well, I saw a number of his movies when I was a little boy—I would say ten years old, and twelve years old, 'cause they occasionally played around in the neighborhood. They were not first-run. But we had so many movie houses in the neighborhood, and there were always programs for kids, and they'd run Chaplin stuff. And when I first saw him I didn't appreciate him, as I learned to do in later years. I just thought, you know, he was another one of those guys doing pratfalls and stuff that didn't interest me very much when I was younger.

At what point did you begin to appreciate him?

When I was in my early twenties and I started to see his movies, his full-length movies, I began to realize how brilliant he really was. First as a performer there was just nothing he couldn't do—whatever you needed to be done, it just seemed he could do it, whether it was roller-skating or, or running or falling or eating food, or fighting in a prize ring. Whatever it was, he just did it so brilliantly and, and I couldn't appreciate that at first. And when I was in my twenties and I was thinking seriously about being a comedian, I began to realize how enormously skillful he was. And when I saw *City Lights* I realized what a deep filmmaker he was, 'cause I felt that that film, you know, said more about love than so many purportedly serious investigations of the subject in either books or films. I was very, very impressed with him, and then, of course, I began to be impressed with the fact that he was such a good actor as well, because the serious side of that movie he handled with legendary brilliance.

In fact, when it became fashionable among film critics and the film community to extol Buster Keaton at the expense of Charlie Chaplin, I felt I was in the minority camp there. I felt that, yes, Keaton's films—the actual film from beginning to end—were probably finer pieces of work, but that Keaton was not nearly as funny a comedian as Chaplin. I mean it was a brilliant, brilliant piece of cinema, [and] when you saw Keaton coming down the street, you know, he was a brilliant executor of his own material. But Chaplin was genuinely funny. When you saw Chaplin coming down the street, he was funny. He was malicious and would wipe his soup off with the guy's beard sitting next to him, and he was a genuinely funny person.

When I make my own movies, sometimes I'll see something and I'll think, my God, Chaplin could do, you know, twenty minutes on that. I mean I always feel lucky if I can find one laugh in it someplace. I just feel, if Chaplin were here, he would do fifteen minutes on this and it would be great. This is just where his genius is. Everything he did, he could make into something and develop it.

And I responded, personally, to the . . . to the more intimate nature of his films, to the fact that he was very much more involved in human emotions and . . . and feelings. He did risk sentimentality and failed a portion of the time. When anyone tries to be sentimental or moving, and they fail at it, you know, you want to strangle them at the time, you have such an adverse reaction to it, and that's the risk you take when you do that as a comedian.

But a portion of the time he didn't fail at it. A portion of the time he got pathos in a genuinely moving way—the extreme example being the end of *City Lights* and that's, to me, a finer achievement, a deeper achievement than all of the moments in the Keaton films, and many of the [other] moments in Chaplin's films. To me that resonates more deeply than anything either of them did—the moments when Chaplin went for seriousness and pathos and brought it off, not those execrable moments.

. . . I don't want to say this, 'cause I don't really mean it in these kind of harsh terms, but it's almost as if I would say

[Keaton's are] "cold works of art." They're not cold. They're better than cold. But they're cooler works of art for me than Chaplin's. And because they're cooler than Chaplin's, I personally don't respond to them as much. But there are many, many people, in fact probably the preponderance of people in the film community, who respond to him more. I mean Pauline Kael always used to say to me how much more she appreciated Keaton than Chaplin. And I understand what she was talking about, but it's a . . . a matter of personal taste. She had small tolerance for any kind of sentimentality, you know. . . . Even when it hit the mark, she was very harsh about it and she liked the cool brilliance of Keaton. Uh, I didn't. It's just a personal apples-and-pears choice. I appreciate Keaton very much, but that little bit of humanness in Chaplin, which sometimes is a weakness of his, and embarrasses all of us, I prefer.

What, if any, direct influence on your work did Chaplin or Keaton have?

When you're starting out I certainly—but I think many people—tend to lean on, imitate, copy, steal from the people that they idolize. When I first started out as a nightclub comedian, I was such a great fan of Mort Sahl's that it crept into me, his delivery crept into me. And it helped me on the one hand, [yet] people would say, "Well, if you could lose that, that influence, you know, you'll have your own personality—but until you do . . ." The same with ten million actors who came after Marlon Brando. When I made *Take the Money and Run,* when

I made *Bananas,* my first couple of pictures, I was very much under the sway of these great film comedians. Of course I'm not now, nor was I then, certainly, competent enough to really bring it off, but I did that Chaplin pathos stuff. I'd be walking the streets and look at some fried eggs in the window hungrily, and hope to get the girl, but not get the girl. You know, I was constantly doing things that I thought were Chaplinesque, because I very much thought that he was the finest maker of comic films.

And then someone pointed out to me, after that first film, they would prefer me to be more Keatonesque than Chaplinesque. I had no image of myself nor any idea what audiences expected. And so when I made *Sleeper* I was, I felt, heavily influenced by Keaton, and Peter Bogdanovich once pointed out the relationship between me and Diane Keaton as—no pun intended—a very Keatonesque one. It was not that I idolized the beautiful girl, like I did with Janet Margolin in *Take the Money and Run,* but it was where I was stuck with this idiot and I was trying to escape and, and, uh, she couldn't get anything right, you know, in the same sense as the little girl in *The General*—Keaton was stuck with her, and she couldn't get anything right. And so I was leaning on, copying, stealing from. I wasn't stealing individual jokes but stealing attitudes and, you know, floundering around, very much influenced by those comedians.

I felt [perhaps] more comfortable in a Chaplinesque mode. [In] a picture like *Purple Rose of Cairo* I felt Mia Farrow's character was more Chaplinesque in the thing. At the end, when she's sitting in the movie theater, I think she's a character who gets some pathos. That's always been a more comfortable fit for me.

She's not a blind girl, but she is a blinded girl, isn't she?

She's a blinded girl, and in the film I did with Sean Penn, *Sweet and Lowdown,* I did have a little mute girl who, who idolizes Sean Penn and, and these are all Chaplinesque influences.

It seems to me that when you're the robot in Sleeper *there's something of Chaplin in the scene.*

Right, I was trying to be that. I was trying to be what I had seen Chaplin do. When I was that robot—and I'm going from memory, I haven't seen the picture in thirty years or something—I remember sitting in the robot repair shop and some guy twisted the head off another robot and that was the kind of structure Chaplin would use. He would, he would be in the dressing room before the prizefight, and, uh, and the guy he was going to fight would knock out the winner of the last fight with one quick punch, and Chaplin would be alarmed that he was going to . . . And I was working in that same mode—these hints from Chaplin, these, these, not motifs but these tricks that Chaplin used. I did try and do things I had seen Chaplin do in my own way, or in my own form. Now, when you think back to that exercise desk in *Bananas* that was a pathetic imitation of Chaplin at the eating machine at the beginning of *Modern Times*—a well worked out, complex visual sequence, executed by genius. I took five minutes and these guys built this cockamamie little exercise desk and I got on it. And so what you wind up with is something that you could clearly trace back to Chaplin but is a pale, pathetic imitation, an awful imitation, of what a great master did. If I were to do that again now—I was just too stupid at the time, I didn't know enough about films or filmmaking—if I was to do it now, you know, I would have those guys build me a desk that looked like a million bucks, I would work it out for days beforehand and get a sequence of built-in gags, which is what Chaplin must have done, at least. But I was working right off the cuff. And so what you get is, you know, nothing very thrilling. But the influence is clearly there. I mean I was imitating a guy I loved.

I get a little whiff out of that of not just Keaton and Chaplin but also of Harold Lloyd, to my eye. I don't know why. Maybe it's totally in my eye.

Um, that is in your eye.

Really?

Yes, uh, because I wore these glasses, and people used to make the Harold Lloyd comparison, um, and the ones that didn't like me would say, "Glasses do not make him a Harold Lloyd."

Now the truth of the matter is I never liked Harold Lloyd. I never found him funny. And so I was never thinking of Harold Lloyd at any point. I just happened to wear these glasses and never thought of Harold Lloyd at any point in my life. He's never been an influence on me or someone that I've really appreciated.

What's the influence on Love and Death? *Had you been reading a lot of Tolstoy?*

I had, of course, always loved the Russian classics, and I was trying to do a film with philosophical content, if you can believe it. And I learned that it's hard to do a film with philosophical content if you're too broad. It's just like people can't see the structure of a film in a broad film, they [also] don't take seriously anything that you might be wanting to say in a comedy. Or any issues you might be wanting to deal with, or little comments you want to make—not desperately profound, or original, but any little serious pretensions you might have in the film go unnoticed, because what gets noticed always is the jokes, the snappers, the one-liners, and the sight gags.

And so *Love and Death* was a film in which I wanted to talk about love and death in a comic way. But I failed to communicate that to an audience because I chose a very broad format to do it in, which is the only format I would have known at the time. And so when people saw the picture, they would accept or reject the picture based on how funny they thought it was. If they liked the jokes they liked the picture. If they didn't like the jokes they didn't like the picture.

And that was a successful picture for me 'cause most of the people did like the jokes. But the substance of the picture—

and you could look at me now and say, "Substance? You must be joking"—that picture is a silly picture. It couldn't have any kind of substance whatsoever, and I understand what you're saying and it's my failure not to have framed the substance in a substantive picture.

But I think of that movie as the first primitive sketch for the Woody movies that were to come. Looking at it now. Maybe not when I saw it the first time, but looking at it in the last couple of weeks. The character you play is somewhat death obsessed. Yet he puts it in common terms.

Well, what I was preoccupied with as a person was the tragedy of life, the fact that in the end you're screwed by death, that death is ever present, that death is a constant companion in one form or another, either on the battlefield or in attempted suicides or in duels, or because you're rejected in, in your love life. And love is futile.

Over the years I've been accused of being either cynical or pessimistic about [death], where I just think I'm realistic, but in a way [*Love and Death*] was so removed from any substance—just silly little jokes about [it]—that any hint of seriousness that might have been in my mind failed to convey itself to the audience. So people haven't over the years gone in there and said, "This was a very funny movie, but there is a kind of, if you notice, a kind of tragic undertone to it. There is a certain sense of the futility of life and the . . . the transience of love and the inconstancy of love and the difficulty of love, and the pathos and tragedy of death and, and how it haunts all

our affairs. . . ." [But] the film was too light and silly [for] anyone [to] respond to that aspect of it. It was my fault.

I think one of the funniest parts of the movie is when your
character is condemned to death and believes, though, that the fix
is in, and that he's not going to be shot by the firing squad. Then of
course he is shot. To me it's funny and it's kind of poignant too.

Well, it was supposed to be funny of course, but it was
supposed to resonate in a more poignant way, and because I
was thinking, of course, of Dostoevsky, who they put up before a firing squad when they had no intention of executing
him, and at the last second he was pardoned. But they just
wanted to scare him. And he was scared. . . .

That experience always resonated with me, 'cause Dostoevsky made it so vivid when he wrote about it. And so I had
that in mind when I was doing it, and I wanted people to recall that and to think how terrifying it is when they're going to
shoot you, or when you know you're going to die. Awareness
of death is such a terrifying thing—when you're aware of
your own imminent death. It's so excruciatingly fearful—
much different, of course, than if you don't know—as Camus
said.

I wanted you to be aware of the enormous terror when
you comprehend your own death, either in the long-term future or the immediate future. But I didn't want to subvert the
laugh.

What was important for me is that the audience laughed.

And then only dimly and vaguely should it—if I was successful, which I don't think I was—should it resonate in their
mind—I mean later, when they're home at night or when
they're sleeping in the middle of the night, and they wake up
and they laugh at the joke—after they're through laughing
and they think for a few minutes, and they think, "Gee, I
wonder what it would be like to be in front of a firing squad
and know that they were going to shoot me in a few minutes?" But as I say, you've got to be more skillful than I was to
achieve that.

In that movie, and we're leading now to Annie Hall, *but in
that movie and in* Sleeper *a kind of a character is developed for
Diane Keaton that I find very interesting, because she is your lifelong close friend and earlier you mentioned giggling at Bob Hope
movies with her. She played in those movies as kind of careless
about love. She's not entirely there for your character. She's got her
own interests. There is a wonderful moment in* Love and Death
*where it's announced that you've been killed and she says, "Oh,
well, let's go eat." I guess* distracted *is the best word for the kind of
character she plays.*

Right. Keaton basically is an actress with a great, great
comic gift. And having known her personally so well, I [was]
able to tap into some of her strengths; so I could write things
for her that I knew she could play well, and she did. I was always astonished by her range, because she could sing and
dance in one thing, and then, you know, play dead serious in

something else. I mean it's really a very, very deep range. And when she plays comedy, out and out, like *Love and Death,* one of her strong areas is that kind of distracted quality that she— I don't know where she's picked it up over the years, but she has picked it up and she plays that character very well.

And it fit in very nicely, because when I made *Sleeper* and *Love and Death* I was trying to get a kind of Buster Keaton–style heroine. I wasn't trying to get a Chaplinesque heroine, where I lose my heart over this good, sweet thing, and all that. I was trying to get someone that you throw your lot in with, and you want to kill her sometimes because she doesn't get it, or she screws up your plans or puts your life in jeopardy. And Diane Keaton could play that very, very well. It's part of something that comes naturally to her.

Annie Hall. *I believe I've heard more than once that you wanted to call it* Anhedonia. *Is that true?*

It's true. Marshall Brickman and I wrote it, and we were thinking of different titles. One title we thought of was taken, so we couldn't use that. And the primary title that we wanted was *Anhedonia,* and we tried to sell *Anhedonia* to United Artists—and again United Artists was never dictatorial. They were always very supportive, but they kept saying, "Please, this is such a nice movie and it's likable. Don't you know, you come out with a movie titled *Anhedonia* and you play this in drive-ins or shopping malls across America, no one will come. They won't know what it means. And if they do find out what it means they'll really hate it." And so, you know, they were very nice people, and we gave in and said, "All right, let's just call it *Annie Hall*."

I was going to mention this before. . . . This question will be a little complicated. You as a young kid loved doing magic tricks, and I guess you did them at local parties in Rockaway or somewhere. And Ingmar Bergman had his magic lantern. I think among people who make movies in a serious way there is always an awareness of the magic elements of movies. The fact that you can shift time and space is the most basic element in it, but there are other tricks too. For example, in Annie Hall *they have a conversation but the subtitles tell what their real thoughts are. Or later they're making love and the Keaton figure gets out of bed and watches. It's a big step ahead in movie-making from your point of view. It's also the first movie, it seems to me, where you're beginning to do something that's so characteristic of your movies—very long takes, like where you and Tony Roberts are walking along the street, and it's really an endless take. I begin to see in that movie the beginning of—you're going to hate me for saying this—your mature style.*

Well, *Annie Hall* was a turning point for me in a few different ways. One is that I wanted to start to do movies that were not just agglomerations of gags.

I wanted to do a movie that might not have anything funny in it for a minute, or five minutes, or something, but you would still not be bored by the movie, you'd still be interested in the characters. And in order to do that I had to sacrifice jokes, giving up things to make a movie that's, in a certain sense, less funny in a way but more character developmental, and with a greater plot to it, or greater emphasis on involvement with the characters. And that's what we tried to do with the script of the movie.

Also it was the first time that I worked with Gordon Willis as a cinematographer, and before that I had not really . . . well, let me put it this way, I learned a lot from him. He's the best American cinematographer, I felt, and a number of other people have felt that way as well. And I was able to learn a certain amount about filmmaking from him. Actually I had two very good teachers. One was Ralph Rosenblum, the editor, whom I worked with for a number of years, who really taught me a lot about editing, and Gordon Willis, who taught me a lot about movies in general, and from a photographic perspective. And so that movie was a turning point for me, both technically and in terms of wanting to do movies where the, the characters and the seriousness of the movie started to compete with the reliance on gags all the time.

It also is a movie, it seems to me, which takes up a theme that later comes up in a lot of your movies—people begin affairs with high passion and high hopes and yet by the end of the movie or by the end of the affair their sexual life is kind of in disarray, and they're bored with each other. The magic has left them, and they're left with the husk of the relationship. The excitement is gone. I don't know if you mean to say that that's part of the anhedonic quality of these particular lives, or whether it's something more universal. I'm thinking of something I read recently—that sexual attraction generally only lasts four years. Anyway, that seems like a big theme for you.

Right. I saw that all around me, and again people always thought I was pessimistic or cynical, but I saw a tremendous amount of exactly that—of relationships that started between men and women, and something would wear out. They started with all good faith, and everybody swore allegiance and great love and fealty and then you looked up in six days, or six months, or six years, or whatever, and everything had somehow come to nothing, or something had gone wrong somewhere. It was more frequent than two people who would meet with good intentions and form a relationship and things would last. That was the rarity.

What we had grown up being taught in Hollywood movies, or what was represented in Hollywood movies, was that at the end you'd live happily ever after. But that didn't seem to be the case. Almost everywhere I looked, it just wasn't the case.

Even in cases of people who stayed together I found, when I looked hard, that they were embittered and angry and compromising in ways that were bothering them, and cheating on each other. As a dramatist, these things became interesting. For someone who could do comedy, it, it made for interesting comedy. The relationships were interesting, and the laughs that emerged out of those . . . those painful situations and those failed situations were, were funny in a way that had a sad component to them and gave the laugh a richness that just a plain topical gag or a crazy gag didn't have.

It seems to me that some of the magical stuff I referred to before is where the best humor is in the movie. I think the whole Hall family in Wisconsin is beyond funny, especially having come from Wisconsin myself. I'm thinking of the moment when Grammy Hall looks over and you're dressed as a Hasidic. That's a great joke, and also a profound joke. There's something oddly touching about it too.

Yes, but that's true. I mean the movie's inherently got a sad quality to it, because it's about a failed relationship. On the level that it most desires, it fails. It settles for a second choice and succeeds on that level. It doesn't end as a contentious, embittered, vitriolic failed relationship—it ends with a nice, warm friendship between two people. So that's . . . that's some kind of redeeming thing. But [they] fail to achieve the relationship [they] hope to achieve.

One of the things that struck me looking at it again is that Alvy pretty much stays where he was at the beginning of the film. His career doesn't appear to have a peak or a valley, while she discovers this gift for singing, and that seems to focus her. I wouldn't say he becomes unfocused, but he doesn't become any more tightly focused.

I think my character remained the same because it became clear to Marshall Brickman and myself, when we were writing the thing, that the potential for character change was all with Keaton's character. Our first draft didn't have much of that, and when we reviewed it we saw we were missing a good bet here, because here's a woman who comes to New York and clearly has the potential for great change and great comic change too. And that's the direction we should move in. So we didn't care much about my character; the rich vein of humor was in Diane Keaton's character—and that's where we decided to put our attention.

That was a movie that was inordinately popular, and yet as I look back on it that seems a little odd to me—because of its wistfulness, its failure to achieve a fully happy resolution. How do you account for the success of that movie?

Well, let me say this: the film was not such a success as, as one might think. When it came out it was well received by the critics, for the most part—though not unanimously so. And it did my usual disappointing business. I mean, it did modest business, nothing great. It was not a picture that came out and automatically and quickly captured the imagination of the public. It had a loyal core following that kept it going in one or two small theaters for a long time.

And it had a, a nice quality, apparently, an appealing quality for people in show business, and so it wound up winning the Academy Award. And only after it won the Academy Award did it start to make some money. Once the imprimatur of the Academy was put on it, and it was reissued, then it started to glean bigger box office—never spectacular. If I'm not mistaken, it was the smallest-earning Academy

Award–winning picture in history to that time, and maybe of all time, I don't know.

The movie has one other aspect to it that you would come back to and develop, and that is this uneasy relationship with celebrity. I think of two things: the first is he's waiting for Annie at the theater and these two goons from New Jersey assault him and want his autograph, because they've seen him on television. They know he's sort of famous, and he's annoyed and anxious with that. Then there's the upside: he's standing in the line at the movie and this terrible, boring, pretentious idiot is going on and on about the movie, and your character has the wish-fulfillment of having Marshall McLuhan step out from behind a poster and clean this guy's clock. It's the beginning of the theme of celebrity in your movies, I think.

Well, celebrity is something that came uneasy to me. I was a writer, and a writer by nature is reclusive. You're isolated. You stay home in a closed room by yourself writing all the time, and you need to survive. And so when I became a performer, and succeeded as a performer, I found myself a celebrity.

I found myself doing a television show, and people would recognize me in the street, and I, personally, had an uneasy time of it. Other performers I knew, other comedians I knew, responded to it in varying ways, some even worse than me. Others were very graceful about it all. They had no problem whatsoever, and they wore their celebrity, they wore their recognition, more gracefully. Some loved it.

I've seen comics walk into a restaurant and yell out something to the whole restaurant and the restaurant suddenly looks up and they begin joking with everybody. That's just their personality. Mine was always a . . . a lack of ease in those circumstances, and so it's probably reflected in my movies down through the years. It's an issue that's made me uncomfortable, and also has an enormous amount of perquisites that in my opinion outweigh the discomforts.

Yes, your life is no longer private, and you're inundated by paparazzi and things are printed in columns and things are said about you and that's the down side, and it's not pleasant. On the other hand, you know, you get very good seats to the World Series, and reservations at the restaurant, and if you call your doctor on a Saturday or Sunday he'll see you. There's a lot of perquisites that a celebrity gets that are wonderful. In the end I think they outweigh the down side of it.

Really? Even after all you've been through?

Oh yes, I do. I do think that the things you gain from celebrity in the final analysis are more beneficial than the things you have to give up.

Then let me leap ahead, to Stardust Memories, *which is a picture I've had to see three or four times before I could really come fully to grips with it, and like it. But I'm wondering—is celebrity the one subject that is in some ways forbidden to celebrities to talk about in an artistic form? That is to say, if you're famous you're not supposed to ever acknowledge your fame by trying to make a work of art out of the issues that arise from it, which I think happened in the response to* Stardust Memories.

I can't see that as valid. A celebrity, a writer, a playwright, or a filmmaker can make a film on any subject, you know, and if, if what he's done, or she's done, is a valid piece of work, a good piece of work, then it's fine, no matter what the subject is. When I made *Stardust Memories,* it was my own personal favorite film that I had made till that time. It was the first film I'd made that I really got rapped on, because people—and this may have been my lack of skill again, I don't know—people felt that what I was saying in the film was that my audience were fools for liking me, that I was demeaning the audience when that's not what I was doing.

I had never felt that way about the audience, and if I did feel that way I would have been too smart to put it in a movie. I wouldn't have done it. But apparently something miscommunicated. I thought when *Stardust Memories* came out—and I'm very critical of my own films, I mean I could really go over my own films and, you know, it would be very hard for me to find anything nice to say—I felt, my gosh, I had an idea and I brought it off, and it looks like what I wanted to do. And I felt very good about it.

But the film in some way communicated to the audience a wrong message, and I can only say that it had to be my mistake, because there's more of them than me and a number of them came away with that impression. So I in some way gave them the wrong idea.

What was your intention with the movie? What were you try-
ing to say in that movie that didn't work or the audience didn't
get?

Well, all I was trying to do was show a person who was a
success, a tremendous success at what he was doing. He's rich,
he lives in a beautiful place, and he leads a typical successful
life, a high-profile life. And they're going to do a retrospective
of his films on a weekend someplace, and this is his life's work,
his accomplishments. And he's in his kitchen and his maid is
going to make him rabbit for dinner. And he hates rabbit.
He's told her a million times. And she says, "Oh, here," and
she puts the dead rabbit on the table. And he looks at the dead
rabbit and [when] he sees the dead creature there, it projects
him into his own psyche, and everything else that takes place
in the picture takes place in his mind.

In other words, that film festival was not really real?

Nothing was real after that. As soon as he sees the dead
rabbit, the next cut he's pulling up at, at the thing, but it's completely unreal. The people are all odd and grotesque and, and
strange, and the questions are strange, and everything that
happens is odd. And he goes back in his life and he sees his sister, and he sees the woman that played his mother on the
screen, and he sees the girlfriend that he's been trying to get
[free of]. And every time we cut to his apartment, the mural
on the wall changes to reflect his emotional state.

And so finally, when the film is over, you've seen a guy

who finds that despite all his success and all his money and all his adulation, [he] knows that he will never be saved from death—that he's mortal, and suffers from, as we learn in the film, what I called Ozymandias Melancholia, a depression over the fact that years from now they will come across your statue in the desert—the rotting statue in the desert—and it will mean nothing.

And he's miserably unhappy despite all his achievements, and you see the various aspects of his life in what I had hoped would be imaginative ways, his failed relationships and his more successful one and his life as an artist—his movies and his fantasies. And in the end, you know, [none of that] saved him, and he . . . he was, despite all his success, a very unhappy person. And people said to me, after they saw the movie, "We're so sick of this guy's complaining. What has he got to complain about? He's got success. He's got money."

And what I wanted to say to them was, "Yes, he does. He's complaining for you." You know, he's fighting your battle. Yes, he's lucky. You're right. He's got success and he's got money, but for every one of him there's twenty million people who don't have any success, and don't have any money, and are very unhappy, and, and he's saying that even for the ones that have the success—the financial success and the career success and the artistic success—whatever you could want, life is still a very, very painful thing.

The phenomenon itself is still just incredibly painful for him and worse for you, because you don't have any money.

When he goes to the movie, he goes to see *The Bicycle Thief* with the woman, and he's saying, "Yes, when you don't have money to eat, that is your first priority. But when you get past that, when you do get some money, when you do achieve something, then you come up against really unsolvable problems, that you can't solve just by accumulating . . . enough money to eat. You come up against existential problems, which are overwhelming."

And so, anyhow, all of this was on my mind when I made it. None of it had any relation, in my mind, to ridiculing my audience, or saying my audience were fools for liking me, or anything like that. It was just the farthest thing from my mind, it would not have occurred to me.

But through my lack of skill I managed to convey that other thought, and not my intended thought, to the audience. I did convey it to some people. I mean, I will say there were a certain number of people who liked that movie, and, and a certain amount written about it that was quite nice. But there were, for the first time, people, a number of people really, [who] got offended and angry. . . .

[But] to me, even after all of that, [even] after the results of the movie were in, I still maintained for years that it was my favorite movie because I was just being honest. I felt I had set out to make a certain kind of movie and I had made it, and whether I had a blind spot or not, I felt it worked. And it might not have worked for everybody in the audience. . . . Maybe it worked for no one but me. But for me it worked just fine, and I got more of a pleasurable feeling out of that movie . . . than with a movie like *What's New, Pussycat?*, which humiliated me yet worked very well for an audience. It was the highest-grossing comedy of its time, but for me a total embarrassment. Whereas *Stardust Memories* I was very proud of, but the audience was annoyed at. So it was an interesting experience.

People keep coming up to this guy, including the aliens from another planet, saying, "We like your work, especially the early funny ones." So that leads me to ask you, are the early funny ones a burden to you? Because you obviously have gone in a lot of new directions since them. But I'm sure people have said to you, "I like the early funny ones." I believe Pauline Kael took that position in her criticism of you. What's your answer to that?

It's never been a real burden. I feel this way about it: I had characters coming up to the character I played in *Stardust Memories* saying, you know, "Uh, can you help me with this? Will you, will you sign this for me? Will you? I have relatives in a concentration camp, can you help me there?" Whatever—I can't remember, it's been so long ago, but everybody had something they needed from him.

They want you to read their scripts, they . . .

Yeah, they all needed something. The business about "I liked your earlier funny movies" was just one of the things that occurred to me that I used a couple of times, and it didn't have extra meaning, or particular personal meaning. It was just something that occurred to me that I thought was amusing, but no more amusing than the other things that people were asking him for. And so I used it, and it rang a bell with people. They thought the character was me—that I didn't like making comedies, that I thought they were foolish for liking the comedies.

But of course none of this had even occurred to me. I feel fine with my early funny movies. They were pleasurable to make, fun to make—*Bananas* and *Take the Money and Run.* I've recently made, you know, *Small-time Crooks* and *The Curse of the Jade Scorpion,* and some years ago I made *Manhattan Murder Mystery.* Those kinds of films are fun to make occasionally, but I would be bored stiff making the same kind of movie all the time. Sometimes I like to make a movie like *Interiors,* sometimes I like to make a movie like *Hannah and Her Sisters* or *Zelig* or a musical just to keep me interested. I like to vary them. I don't put any great value on one over the other.

You know, if you ask me, I think most of the films I've made, almost all the films I've made, are very wanting, and I don't have a tremendous opinion, a tremendously high opinion of them. I did the best I could at the time, and I put them out to the audience and hoped they'd like them. But I have no pronounced feelings about "the early funny ones." That was something that didn't resonate in my life because I wrote it for a character in a film and it was an easy joke, and it turned out to be a joke that people tuned in on very much. You know, there have been a couple of jokes in my life where that's happened [that] were just casual jokes.

What's another one?

Well, once when I was publishing my book of collected *New Yorker* pieces, they sent me the copy for the back of the jacket—the about-the-author [blurb]. And they had written this thing that was so glowing about me—he did this, and he achieved this, and he directed these films, and he's written this—and you would have thought they were speaking about, you know, Einstein and Leonardo da Vinci. I mean it was amazing.

And so at the end I just penciled in "His one regret in life is that he is not someone else," which I thought, you know, considering . . . I just wrote it in for a joke at the end. Well, they printed it, which was fine and correct and funny. But a thousand times in my life I've been asked seriously by people, "I, I know you want to be somebody else, and who do you want to be? And why do you want to be somebody else? And what's wrong with your life?" You know, to me it was just a casual joke, just like my early funny ones was a, a casual joke for me in the movie. And that has happened to me [constantly]. Once some young people were talking to me about being playwrights. And I said to them that most people strike out by never really writing a play. People want to write a play, and they talk about it and talk about it, [but] they never really write it. I said, "Once you write a play you're more than halfway home." And I said, "You know, 80 percent of life is showing up, just showing up."

Well, I said it in a casual way—just to make a point. [But] that quote has been used ten thousand times all over the world to represent some kind of profound insight, as if I could determine the percentage and meant it as anything more than just a little advice to some playwrights who I felt should write their plays because you don't want to strike out by not writing your play. You want to write a play and let it be a bad play, but not strike out by never writing your play. So these things come back to haunt me, [as] that one did.

But no, I have no negative feelings about my early funny movies, or no great positive feelings about them, and no negative or positive feelings in any great pronounced way about any of my films. I mean, I do what I have an idea for at the time. I'm generally disappointed by the outcome of the film. Many times I get lucky and the audience is generous with me, or the critics are generous. Sometimes they're not. [But] on the whole they've been more generous than ungenerous. And I've had a life in film. But, you know, it's no big deal.

Could you repeat what you just told me off-camera? It was very interesting.

Well, when I did *Stardust Memories* I myself sensed an ambivalent feeling that the public had toward celebrities. In *Stardust Memories* there's this guy that comes up to me and is telling me how much he loves me, and he's such a fan of my work and all of this. Later when I meet him in the movie he shoots me.

And this was a good six months before John Lennon had that same tragic experience. You know, if you're a celebrity, you feel that intensity from the fans, and . . . this intensity has an unreal quality to it, and an ungrounded quality. It doesn't reflect a logical adoration of you or the merits of your work. It's got a different component, and that component pushed an inch the other way often turns out to be violent.

In poor John Lennon's case, the guy loved him and loved him and loved him, and wound up shooting him. And in my movie, which preceded that, that's exactly as I portrayed it, that the guy loved me and loved me and worshiped me, but shot me in the end. And if you're not a celebrity, if you're not familiar with the, the ambivalent feeling when they're mobbing you, when certain people are writing you and pressing themselves on you, it's hard to quite grasp that. But it's known, and many times you'll hear a celebrity say after they're adored and loved by the crowd and everything, they'll finally get [away] and say, "Boy, that was scary." They sense quite correctly, uh, an odd feeling people have toward celebrities.

That raises a point. You are not just an actor, because an actor can say well, that's just a role I play. You most often play roles that you yourself wrote and you yourself directed, so that probably increases the confusion of people between who you are in fact and who you are on the screen. If they're not too bright they may really think you are exactly the person you play on the screen. You've kind of upped the stakes in a way, don't you think?

I think that people have always felt, or wanted to feel at least, that the person they see on the screen in general bears some kind of resemblance to the real-life person. They would have been very upset if they had learned that John Wayne was, you know, a coward, meek and effeminate and completely antithetical to his image on the screen. Just as it would be a terrible thing if you learned that about Clint Eastwood. That's not what you want to think about him.

You think you know some of these people. [But] I remember seeing them on talk shows over the years, where they would say, they'd go into a bar and a guy would pick a fight with them, and say, "I don't think you're so tough." And you'd say, "Hey, I'm an actor, you know. I, I'm just acting." But people want to think that sexy women are sexy offstage, that the macho guys are macho, that the comedians are funny offstage, and it's not exactly as simple as that. There are some elements that are the same, but they're not the same characters really.

There are cases where many elements are the same. But as a rule just as often, if not more often, they're not the same people. And so I've always been in that situation in spades, because I write my movies and unlike Charlie Chaplin, say, who puts on a, a moustache and a hat and a coat and a cane, and looks totally different than the Charlie Chaplin who shows up at the studio to direct a film, I dress in real life the way I dress, 'cause I play a guy from New York, 'cause I have no acting range.

I can't do what Dustin Hoffman does, or Robert De Niro does. I don't have that kind of talent. I play a guy who lives in New York, or who sounds like he lives in New York, who's not believable as the chief of police, who's believable in a certain number of things, and has a certain limited range. That I can do, and I can do that decently well, but I can't go beyond that. And so I wear my own clothes, and I sound like me, and I wear these glasses, and I look like me.

But over the years I've always said that there is some similarity [between me and my characters], but there's great dissimilarity really, and the plots of the movies, the stories of the movies, are fabrications. They're fabrications by me. Or they're fabrications by me in collaboration with Marshall Brickman, or Mickey Rose, or Douglas McGrath, with whom I wrote *Bullets over Broadway.* You know, they're not autobiographical tracks.

And it's possible, if people understood that, they would not come to see me at all. I think they're getting the pleasure out of me as a comedian and the pleasure that . . . that I have something to offer as an entertainer. But, in fact, the most pleasure they're getting is some kind of odd identification with me as a character in life and in film, where they overlap to a great degree, and they're not quite sure who's me and who's not me, and are these stories true, and do I really feel that way, and did this really happen?

And so . . . after *Annie Hall* people thought that I grew up in Coney Island and that's how I met Diane Keaton and that's how we parted, and that my father ran a concession at Coney Island. They think the actual details of the story are true, when in fact they're not true. They're fabrications. There are some similarities, and I understand why they feel that way, but the scary thing to me is that unintended by me, the pleasure I may be giving them and have given them over the years is in direct proportion to how much they identify that screen character with me as an actual person in life.

Well, I think your most profound meditation on celebrity is Zelig, *because this is a character with no character. I think somebody in the movie says, "Well, as far as I can see all he wanted to do was be liked." That is his salient and perhaps only characteristic. But it is a spectacular movie, first of all in its technical brilliance, the matching of old newsreels to contemporary stuff. Nobody's ever done that better than you do in that movie. But also the notion of a man who really isn't there, and is there only as an image, and becomes famous for this weird talent of being able to project himself into newsreels and still photographs with famous people. That is the antithesis of what you've just said about celebrity, but to me it's profound. I don't know how you read that movie, or maybe I'm reading it wrong.*

You're reading that movie correctly. I think that was one of my more successful movies. And it was a movie where I think the content of the movie, which you are picking up on and talking about, was overshadowed by the technical work on the movie. So, yes it was hard and all of us labored to make that documentary look like a real documentary. Sandy Morse, the editor, and Gordon Willis, the photographer—we all worked very hard to make that happen, and we learned how to do it as we went along. I realized as I was going through it that I didn't want real actors in it—that real people sounded the right way, and real actors didn't sound the right way. And there were many things we learned during the course of making it.

But the . . . the real reason I made that movie, what interested me, was the kind of person that I felt was ubiquitous, the kind of person who assimilated into every group because he or she wanted to be liked, and was a different person to every different group he was with. I've seen people . . . you'll see them . . . they'll be discussing something very simple. They'll be discussing a film and they'll say, "Oh, well, I, I didn't like, you know, the last James Bond film. I thought it was, uh, very foolish and silly." And then they'll be speaking with someone else, and the other people will lead by saying, "We saw the James Bond film. We loved it. We thought it was great," and this person suddenly will shift and say, "Yeah, that had some exciting things in it. It really did have some wonderful special effects," and they're suddenly abandoning their own principles and abandoning their own persona—so that they don't cause waves, they don't cause ripples, and they're liked by the other person.

Now, when you extrapolate this to its nth degree, what you wind up with is fascism, because that's who those people were. They gave up everything, they gave up all their own feelings to be led by this hypnotic leader. They just—when you give up your own personality just to be liked, so as not to make waves, that's what fascism and tyranny thrive on and what they're all about.

And I . . . so I wanted to make the movie about that. And in the course of it the guy was a national celebrity, he just automatically became sensational—everything he did caused a sensation. People wanted to pay to see him. It was an amazing phenomenon. When you commercialized that phenomenon, it gave him celebrity status. But it was really just a sad defense mechanism, predicated on the fact he never wanted to say that he had not read *Moby Dick,* and wanted to fit in with the group and say, "Oh yes, I read it. I liked it very much," and, and keep going with the crowd.

Now, it became so profound in him that eventually he was a phenomenon all over the world, for decades.

Is most celebrity just that? An actor, for example. However great the actor is, is he just someone who wants to be liked? It would be true of politicians too. Most of them are worthless. But they feed on the fact that people think there's something great about them. Are we saying that nine-tenths of celebrity is a total fraud, that everybody's a Zelig who's to a degree famous, especially famous for not doing something that's concrete, like painting a picture or writing a poem?

Well, no, no, I wouldn't say that. I would say that most people who are celebrities and continue to be celebrities, you know, have some kind of legitimate contribution to make. And even the fly-by-night celebrities, at least for a moment have some little cheap contribution to make to the culture, uh, that's either fun or amusing—you know, a little buzz for a second.

Occasionally you get an unjustified celebrity, where—uh, and I really got into this more in my movie *Celebrity*—where it became apparent that *everybody* was achieving celebrity status, whether he was a plastic surgeon or a clergyman on television, or, uh, Charles Manson, or whoever it might be. All of a sudden the country was hyperaware of celebrity as a phenomenon, and it worked magically. I mean you could be the best plastic surgeon in the world, but the guy who got the layout in *Time* magazine or *Newsweek* as *the* plastic surgeon, the *celebrity* plastic surgeon, was the guy who went through the roof with it.

I think most celebrities, you know, do something to achieve that status—they make some kind of contribution, and even Zelig made a minuscule contribution. But occasionally you get one who's able to maintain celebrity for a surprising amount of time, based on very little, based on really a very small contribution. But that's a rarity, I think.

Since we're on this group of films, let's just briefly talk about Celebrity. *The thing that to me is most interesting in the movie is the crossing of those two—there's one guy who desperately wants celebrity, and there's this woman who's brilliantly played by Judy Davis . . .*

Yeah, she's great.

. . . who doesn't want celebrity. And she gets the celebrity and he doesn't get it, and that last line of hers—"Gee, I hope you catch a break"—that's resonant.

Right. Oh, I've always been a firm believer that there's a certain number of things in life that just cannot be tackled head on, no matter how much you try. Love, you know, a good relationship, is one, and celebrity would be another one. There are a few. There's a big element of chance involved in it. You really do need a break. Another one of my—you know, I'm a compendium of crackpot theories, I have no compunction about putting them in my films—is [that] I'm a big believer in luck. It appears in all my movies.

I . . . I feel that luck is the chief component in a good relationship between a man and a woman, and that luck guides our lives much more than we care to admit. Coming out of an age of psychoanalysis, people tend to not feel that way. They tend to feel, "I'm in control." And you hear guys say, "Well, heck, I make my luck, you know, I don't . . . I don't depend on luck," or, or "You've got to work at a relationship." I, personally, my observations in life have not been that. I . . . I don't feel that's what does it.

I feel that really luck plays a much greater role—a frightening role in our lives—than we care to admit. We would like to feel that we have more control, and, you know, it's good that we strive to gain control, and so things like psychoanalysis—to the degree that it can help one gain some control in life, if it does—that's great. But in the end it's really luck that dominates a large part of our life.

And in *Celebrity,* you know, that comes out in a certain way. I certainly feel it in terms of the couple—that he wants nothing more than to be famous and get his script done and try and try and try, and she just inadvertently stumbles into it because the breaks fall her way. Now, can you extrapolate from that—what's the point of working? Just sit there and sit back. No, not as simple as that. You do have to work, but—and I exaggerated it for the purpose of making my point in the movie—luck is going to play a bigger part in it than you'd like it to play.

There's another aspect of that movie—that he's such a schmuck, the Kenneth Branagh character. In other words, his luck would be fine if he didn't have to go off with the Winona Ryder character. He's got a perfectly nice woman who then turns on him and destroys what might have been his luck—his novel, which apparently isn't so bad. But he cannot contain his sexual restlessness, and that is not entirely uncharacteristic of a number of other males, and a few females, in your other movies. Does that make any sense? He's really, literally, fucking up, is what I'm sensing about this guy.

Well, you know, one's relationships are not rational. I mean, I just see it all around me. The guy in *Celebrity,* Kenneth Branagh, has got a perfectly beautiful woman dying to move in with him, he's on the verge of starting a new relationship that's meaningful. But in the end, all that's logic on paper.

That's like, on paper the Seattle Mariners should have beaten the Yankees, but they didn't, because there's another element involved.

And that other element is that there's something inside his heart, some irrational impulse, that wants Winona Ryder. It may even be that down deep he's got a brilliant, intuitive sense that she's going to hurt him, and that she's not going to be there for him, and that it's not going to work with her, and that he really doesn't want it to work.

So he scuttles the relationship with Famke Janssen. He scuttles that relationship and he goes right to the one that some lifelong instinct tells him is not going to work. And he'll be off the hook. It won't be his responsibility. He'll go with her and she'll be the one that screws up and he'll be able to say, "My God, this girl was great. I gave her everything I had, and she, she just screwed it up"—when in fact he picked her for exactly that reason. That could have been what was on the mind of the character that Kenneth was playing.

Or it could have been that he was just hopelessly in love with Winona and didn't sense that she would hurt him, and sort of naively hoped that this would be it, 'cause his heart—even though all the logic said go with the other girl—his heart was with Winona, and he went with her and got screwed. I don't really know myself. But I know that I see it all around me.

Let's go back to a movie that I didn't like particularly when I first saw it, and which I liked a lot when I saw it this time. That's

Interiors. *It seems to me the big theme, which surfaces in that movie and will come up again certainly in* Manhattan, *is very simple—you just want a relationship that will work. And all of these people are chattering and nattering about this and that, and okay, it's interesting, but they're not focusing on their own happiness and their own relationships. It seems to me that in a lot of your movies there's a sort of upper-middle-class buzz that interferes with the best things in life, if you will, and that family is in particular prone to that kind of buzzing. The only person who's simple and direct and loving is the Maureen Stapleton character—and everyone has contempt for her, with the exception of E. G. Marshall. And that notion of this frantic, buzzing pseudo-intellectual community that just can't get to the heart of the matter seems to be in a lot of your movies.*

Well, of course I observe that a lot. I mean, maybe it's the people I've known. Shall I speak about that movie for a moment?

Yes, please do.

I had a few clear-cut things that I wanted to convey in it, and conveyed them to the best of my ability at that time. I wanted to show three sisters. First off, one who was genuinely gifted—that is Diane Keaton, who is a writer—and who based everything in her life on art, who put all her faith in art, and had come to the realization that art was not going to save her. In the end you can be the most profound artist, you can be Picasso, and, you know, you may live to be a hundred or something, but sooner or later it's over. And art doesn't save you, and the notion of posterity, of achieving immortality through posterity, is the artist's Catholicism. It's the, the artist's sense of an afterlife, which I don't believe in, at all. Catholics do believe in an afterlife. I don't. And artists believe in an afterlife, which I feel is equally fallacious. So that was Keaton.

Mary Beth Hurt was someone who I wanted to design as a character who's full of feelings but has no artistic talent at all, which is a terrible position to be in in life—to have intuitive feelings about life and nature and suffering and human beings and love, and have no way to express them—not being able to draw or paint or write or compose or get these feelings out in any way.

The other girl was the sister who went to California, and she was just supposed to represent kind of an empty sensuality—as one of the characters said, "form without content"—just an empty kind of person who had gone off and was attractive, but there was nothing there, just superficial physical beauty.

These daughters were victimized by this mother who was psychotic and intensely dedicated to aesthetics, just intensely dedicated at the expense of the whole family. Her particular aesthetic was severe and restrained and everything was rigidly tasteful. One got the feeling that the ashtray had a number on it, and you'd put it down on a corresponding number on the

table, that nothing could be moved, everything had to be perfect. She was trying to arrange the world in an ordered, perfect, beautiful, low-key fashion.

And into this [situation] comes this vulgarian, Maureen
Stapleton, who likes her steaks blood rare and is completely
antithetical to everything that the daughters have been
brought up to respect and value. She sits at the table and, if
you'll notice, does magic tricks, 'cause for me reliance on
magic is really, I think, the only way out of the mess that we're
in. If we don't get a magical solution to it we're not going to
get any kind of solution, and that ties in with my feeling about
luck playing a very big part [in life]. You really do need some
magic or you're not going to make it. And she's going to take
the father away, which has a certain oedipal annoyance to the
daughters anyhow, and they just find her the, the antithesis of
their mother in taste and restraint. And the mother kills herself and the daughter tries to save her and drowns and dies.
And the new mother [Stapleton's character] gives her mouth-
to-mouth resuscitation.

*There's the attempted suicide, and the daughter attempts to
save her and almost dies in the process.*

Yes, Mary Beth Hurt drowns and she dies and, and Maureen Stapleton gives her mouth-to-mouth resuscitation and
brings her back to life. And it's really a second birth from a
new mother, from a more legitimate mother. And one hopes
at the end of the picture that these daughters will experience
now, with a new mother, some kind of warmth that will

change their lives to some degree. Whether that happens, I don't know.

So there's a tiny bit of hope at the end of that movie?

Just a tiny, tiny bit, the barest bit. Certainly maybe a little bit for Mary Beth Hurt. Probably Keaton and the other girl are beyond being helped.

To me this movie relates to Manhattan, *oddly enough. It seems to me that the conflict in* Manhattan *is between the Keaton character and this sweet seventeen-year-old girl, who is offering your character the simplest, best thing in the world, pure love. And your character rejects that—granted in an ambiguous way— before at the end coming back to her, possibly too late. It seems to me the most fundamental of conflicts in your movies, between people who offer what Maureen Stapleton offers in* Interiors *and all these other people who are putting down Mahler and Bergman and other artists you admire and are full of complicated ideas that really add nothing to their sum of happiness. Isn't that a fundamental issue in a lot of your movies?*

It is fundamental in that there are these high-strung, complex, intellectual people who find it very, very hard— impossible—to have good relationships with the other sex because they're so finely tuned, and have so much difficulty getting pleasure out of life, and are so critical of everything. They are smart, and they do have ideas about everything and strong feelings about everything, and very neurotic feelings about many aspects of life. So when someone comes along like

Mariel Hemingway, who's just, you know, too young to be spoiled, too completely simple and sweet and nice, the character that I was playing in the movie couldn't appreciate her.

Instead he falls for the annoying pseudo-intellectual—or probably intellectual to some degree—Diane Keaton. He instinctively, or habitually, has learned to go for that kind of woman, to go for the neurotic, difficult, complicated woman, and . . . and not see the forest for the trees, not see that right in front of him is really somebody he would be happy with, if he can just get rid of all this civilization that's weighted on his shoulders.

It's crossed my mind to start my film of this interview not with any actor but with the close-up of the tape recorder in which your character is saying, "Idea for a short story . . . ," and then he starts making a list of the simple pleasures in his life that makes it meaningful for him. Is that as close as you've come to stating a philosophy of life in one of your movies?

Well, the general overall philosophy I have stated in my movies, inadvertently it seems, strikes people as pessimistic, gloomy, and they often use the word *cynical.* I never see it that way. I think that I'm either realistic or naively upbeat, but they don't see it that way. In *Manhattan* I felt that I was sort of upbeat at the end. The guy comes to realize that the young girl is really the one he should have been with all the time, and by the time he gets to her it's probably a little bit too late. She's probably on her way into the world, and not really going to [come back to him].

So people will say well, gee, that's a very cynical way to think, or a very pessimistic way to think, but I don't see it as pessimistic, I see it as unfortunately realistic. I, myself, found the biggest weakness with a film like *Hannah and Her Sisters* was the ending of the picture. The original ending was supposed to be that Michael Caine has been in love with Hannah's sister all the time, and Hannah's sister gets tired of waiting around for him, and she marries some other guy. And he is despondent, but goes back with Hannah to live his life out with Hannah in a way that is a second choice, and he'll always long for the sister, and see her at little family parties, but never be able to have a relationship with her again, and always be stuck with his second choice for life.

That was my original ending. When I put that picture together, and that ending was as I just described it, it was such a downer. It was like the picture . . . just fell off the table.

And so I had to put a more upbeat ending on the picture, because I just had not justified that level of sort of Chekovian sorrow. So I put in the ending that *Hannah* has.

But at least your character and the Dianne Wiest character get together. It's kind of nice. It's sweet.

Yes, I felt the ending was upbeat. And I think, in general, you know, there's a modicum of hope someplace. Even at the end of *Purple Rose,* when Mia goes back into the movie theater and starts watching the Fred Astaire movie, at least you get the feeling that at the very minimum she's not going to kill herself. She's going to lose herself in escapist films. I'm not Pollyannish, but I don't think I'm cynical or gloomy or pessimistic.

I'd like to go into Hannah and Her Sisters *a little more. It's that cut of New York life. For example, there's the gloomy artist, the Max von Sydow character.*

Not good.

Not good. They are all measuring out their lives in coffee spoons, as it were. But I didn't quite follow what you said about the ending being gloomy and downbeat, because isn't the ending of the film the one you've just described? I mean, the Michael Caine character does go back to his wife, right?

Right, but with not as much disappointment as I originally had. Uh, it, it isn't as sad as I had originally made it. But as you were pointing out, the seminal relationships that run through the picture are men and women who don't seem to come together very successfully for too long because they're inundated by excess baggage that cripples them.

I'd like to pick up on something you said before, which is if we have any hope in this life, it's for magic. And the movie that seems to me to state that most directly is Alice. *Here's this woman who's, once again, overprivileged and rich and all that stuff, but she goes to this weird doctor in Chinatown and the next thing you know she takes a potion and she can fly across Manhattan, and she takes another potion and she can disappear. In fact, she finds a solution in magic eventually.*

Yes.

She finds a life that is agreeable to her and useful to society and has nothing to do with these other people. Could you talk about the function of magic in the particular context of Alice?

Well, you know, the, the whole phenomenon of existence has got a magical quality to it. It's some kind of unexplainable thing like a trick that you . . . you can't get your mind around. Rather than a trick, maybe I should say a grim joke. The only way you're going to [avoid] it is if there's some magical solution—something has got to come along that's magical that lifts you out of everyday reality.

Because as long as you're mired, as we all are, in everyday routine and reality, we're all going to come to the same nasty end, and have the same grim lives. You know, someone with a longer perspective, someone looking at us, we'd look like a bunch of ants on a log, running around. And every hundred years, you know, it's like somebody flushes the toilet and the entire planet is changed. Everybody, all the people you're concerned with now and all the problems you have and all the terrorists and the people that give you a hard time, and the relationships with women that you're pining over, and the husbands that have deserted their wives—all that, all gone.

Every single person—it's a total washout after a hundred years. So unless something comes along that, that we don't know about, that is truly magical, I don't see any real way out of a sad situation.

But that's a wonderful device, the Chinese doctor and his herbs. How did you happen to come to that device? It's a great gimmick, I think.

Alice goes to this doctor, and the problems that are ailing her are not problems that can be dealt with with real medicines, with Western medicines, and they're not problems that can be dealt with, really, with psychoanalysis. I mean, probably she has tried psychoanalysis, but what she needs is magic, and this guy offers it. She really needs somebody that will come in and, and do things of a wondrous nature for her, otherwise she's going to go along in that same life she has—going to the beauty parlors, and shopping for clothes, and, you know, not really living with her husband, who's cheating on her. She really needs a magical transformation. And this is the one guy that can do it for her.

There is also in that movie—and it's the same actor, Joe Mantegna, who plays the same sort of part in Celebrity—*who does represent a realistic alternative. He's just a nice supportive guy. Is that type so rare that he's magical?*

Well, uh, yeah. I mean Joe's got a lot of good stuff going for him—apart from the fact that he's a good actor. He's got a good look and he's got sex appeal, and he projects, he projects a nice feeling for women. I mean, he was a marked contrast. Bill Hurt was playing the part of a, a kind of cold, Wall Street broker—just cheating on his wife and interested in business. Whereas Joe was an artist, he was a musician, and he's got, he's got a built-in warmth—and the same thing in *Celebrity*. He's a guy that Judy Davis is waiting for the other shoe to drop on, and, you know, it never drops, 'cause there is no other shoe to drop. She's the neurotic one, and she makes the problem. She'd be very lucky to wind up with Joe, as would Alice.

There's another movie, Shadows and Fog, *that has a magical element to it. This guy steps through the mirror, and at least temporarily escapes the peril that's pursuing him?*

Magic is the key factor in *Shadows and Fog,* because what I wanted to make was a kind of German expressionist movie, where this homicidal figure was wreaking havoc and causing various reactions to him—the scientific reaction, the intellectual reaction, the overreaction by mobs of vigilantes, the religious fanatic reaction—all, all reactions that we use to cope with death and evil and violence, none of which really work out very well.

And finally, in the end, the only thing that really saves him is a magician with a magic trick, because short of a magical solution there does not seem to be any way out of this terrible existence that we live in.

It's like we're all checkmated, and unless somebody can find a move that will relieve us, that will free us from the checkmate, then we . . . we've had it. And I, I think if it's not magical, it's not going to happen, because all the other solutions I see around me—religious solutions, scientific solutions, intellectual solutions—you know, everything is too little too late and not good enough, and all the things that are in the eyes of writers and poets are not redeemingly effective. They're not good enough. They may say well, it's too bad, it's the best we can do. And I'm saying I agree with you, it's the best you can do, but it's not good enough, and what you really need is some kind of magic. Unless something comes along that's not known to us now, but that is revealed to us, some kind of magical thing, you're going to be stuck with your "This is the best we can do," or "I'll always live on in posterity," or a few nice words at a eulogy, or "He raised some nice children," or "Look at this shelf of books he wrote." Whatever it is, what does it mean? That we all sing the praises of, uh, Mozart? We all sit over his grave and sing his praises? It doesn't mean anything.

You know, if we're to be saved, it's got to be something that we don't know about now, and it's none of the things that are offered up by the authority figures—the politicians, the scientists, the artists—all the people we rely on to save us from our fate. They have not been able to do it, and they can't do it. Now, this is not to say, as I said in *Stardust Memories,* that because science can't solve everything and answer all our problems that it's not a good thing, because it does do some wonderful things. But in terms of the real ultimate source of horror to the human race, we are in search of some kind of magical solution.

Let me just quickly ask, as a little kid doing magic tricks did you sense the magic in magic? That there was some transformative power there that offered a little hope or whatever for you? Because that same kid who was doing magic tricks is also the same kid— that hilarious scene in Annie Hall *where he's taken to the doctor and he starts talking about the infinite nature of the universe and all that, implying of course that the doctor, the man of science, can't cure what ails him.*

Well, I was, as a kid, very interested in magic, but I was interested in the aesthetics of it. I mean, to me all the beautiful silk handkerchiefs and chromium canisters and billiard balls and things looked wonderful. There is in that some sense of the religious or some sense of there's hope for something other than what we know as real. That is, when you see a magic trick it's something that defies reality.

You know, my way has been movies. I live for a year in a movie. I write the movie. I live with those characters. I cast the movie. I'm on the set. The set is maybe a 1940s nightclub, or maybe it's a contemporary thing, but I live in a fake world for ten months. And by living in that world I'm defying reality in a way—or at least hiding from reality. But that's what it's all about for me.

Really? That's the impetus for the work?

To me that's the impetus for the work. For me—I've said this before—it's like a patient in an institution who they give basket weaving to, or finger painting, because it makes him feel better. The actual work of making the film is great for me, because I get to create a fake situation and live in that situation and act the character, or if I'm not in the film live with those characters and bring them to life, and dress them, and put music around them, and put them in a setting that we create, and manipulate them. I control the reality for that period of time, and live amongst beautiful women and guys who are brilliant and guys who make witty remarks or who are extra brave. And it's great.

Therefore, when a film comes out, if it does well at the box office I'm thrilled. If it doesn't do well, you know, I . . . I'm disappointed, but not crushed. If the critics like it, I'm delighted. If they don't like it, I'm disappointed but not crushed. Because for me the big thing is the making of the film. If I've spent ten months making a film and I've enjoyed the ten months of fantasy, of living in my dream world, then what happens to it [is not important]. I'll always root for its success, but I . . . I can live if it's not [successful]. The important part is over for me.

So you're not a workaholic then? Because the book on you is well, Woody, he's got to make a picture every year, and it has never quite fitted what I've known of you.

I'm not a workaholic—that's a big myth about me. I, I don't work frantically and fanatically. I work very casually. I'm lazy. Films are not my first priority. I play my clarinet. I enjoy that. I go to ball games. I watch television. I mean I watch sports on television a lot. I like to spend time with my family. When I make a film, if I don't have it too great, but could make one more shot, and it's six o'clock at night, and I've got to be at Madison Square Garden for the Knicks at seven, I blow the shot off and go to the Knicks game, all the time. I mean films are not a religion with me.

I like the work. It's fun work in the same sense that it's fun to go out and play softball or some guy has fun going out on his boat or something. And, you know, it keeps me sane to the degree that I'm sane. It helps me. But I'm not a workaholic. I don't work frantically at all. I could do more than I'm doing if I wanted to.

*Let me ask this. To me this is one of the strangest of your movies—*Another Woman. *Gena Rowlands is in the foreground—the central figure—and she is kind of like you as you describe yourself. She's trying to lose herself in—in her case—intellectual activities. But not succeeding as well as you seem to when you're working on a movie. And she's entirely surprised by the waywardness of the life around her. It startles her. Is that what that movie is about?*

What that movie is about is a woman who is cold and intellectual and bright, and doesn't want to know the truth about her life, is not interested in the truth, and has blocked it out. Her husband's cheating on her. She has blocked that out. She's cold. She's cold to her brother. She's not had a close relationship with her father. All of this she doesn't want to know about and doesn't want to face. And finally she reaches a point in life where she gets to be middle-aged, and the truth encroaches upon her.

She gets a room where she's isolated, where she can work,

and the truth starts coming in through the wall to her, through some kind of anonymous psychiatric patient who is really some version of her, and no matter how much she's blocked off the truth, it's coming right through the wall to her, and she can't put up walls anymore. . . . And so as the truth starts to become known to her, she starts to get more and more involved—she follows the woman patient, and she gets more interested, and she starts to learn about herself and what a cold fish she is and what an empty life she's had.

Gena Rowlands was such great casting. I love the contrast between her calm and reasonable voice-over narration and the increasing panic and desperation of her behavior.

Well, she's great. I mean, you know, I just felt if I could get her to do it. . . . She's one of those actresses that can do anything. So you're always better off, I've found over the years, with a great actor or actress. Even if they're not completely right for the part, they'll give you what you want sooner than a mediocre one who [may be] more naturally correct for the part.

Could we turn to Crimes and Misdemeanors? *Whatever the critics thought of it at the time, I find that people often mention it to me as something like a masterpiece among your later films. In any case, it's a very interesting movie in that it has this comic level going along with this dark story of a man who is willing to murder to keep his secrets and his status in life. It's a very complex movie.*

I had two fairly simple points that I wanted to make with

the movie. First off, I wanted to make a movie that was serious and also comic. I got to a point where I liked the idea of combining comedy [with] serious material, because it was interesting to me, for my—uh—activity for the year. The story with myself and Mia and Alan Alda was about [the idea] that good intentions in life don't mean a thing. I mean, they do in your heart—but to society, success is the bottom line, and for all my good intentions I was a loser.

I wanted to make a documentary, I wanted to do this noble thing. And nobody cares—it just didn't mean a thing. But Alan Alda was a success, and because he brought in the bucks and because he was a success, they wanted him to lecture at colleges. He might have been lecturing on sitcoms on television, but they afforded him intellectual status and he was a success with women. In the end the bottom line is, if you make money, if you're successful, people will accord you intellect and, and they'll forgive all your errors, all your faults. In our society, good intentions don't mean anything if you're not a success.

In the other story, with Marty Landau, I just wanted to illustrate in an entertaining way that there's no God, that we're alone in the universe, and that there is nobody out there to punish you, that there's not going to be any kind of Hollywood ending to your life in any way, that your morality is strictly up to you.

If you are willing to murder and you can get away with it, and you can live with it, that's fine. People commit crimes all the time, violent crimes and terrible crimes against other people in one form or another, and they get away with it and they can live with it. . . .

So Marty Landau hires somebody to kill his mistress. But his character [does not] degenerate, and he's [not] caught in massive guilt and nightmares—not at all. He goes on—the police do not detect him—he goes on to live a perfectly normal, upper-middle-class life, and no God is going to suddenly descend and throw him into hell or strike him with lightning. If he wants, if he makes the moral choice, if he wants to turn himself in, he can do that. He didn't make that moral choice—he made the choice that he wants to do it and get away with it, and he did it and got away with it. And, and that's the world we live in.

He does endure a certain fear of being caught.

For a while he does. He fears being caught for a while. But once that fear blows over, by the time the wedding comes around in the last scene, the boat has sailed. The police have given up on it. You know, it's dropped into the dustbin of unsolved crimes.

Sure, he's scared at first. When the detective comes to his office and they're asking him questions, he's nervous. But once it passes, it passes—and just like the thousands or millions of crimes that are committed all the time in the world, there's no retribution for it, and no justice done. And . . . and so I was merely saying—and now I'm making a case against myself as being pessimistic—I was really saying, there's no God and no justice.

There's a yearning for God in the film, I think. Marty Landau feels it. Even in the discussion at the very end of the picture between your character and Marty, you sense that yearning.

Yes, there is. We wish that we lived in a world where there was a God and where these acts would be adjudicated in some way. But we don't. And Marty, if he had his choice, yes, would rather live in a world—before he committed his crime—would rather live in a world where there was a God, or where there was some kind of justice, and then maybe he wouldn't have committed his crime, maybe he wouldn't have done it.

But he lives in a world where it's simply up to you to, to make your moral choices. And if you can get away with it, you get away with it. Just like at the Seder scene in the movie, where they're saying that history is written by the winners, and if the Nazis had won World War II, our history books would look very different today. You would not get the same history books that you have now. They didn't win, fortunately.

There are several points in this movie that I think are very interesting. There are two people who as characters keep a kind of purity in it. One is the niece, and she seems entirely untouched by evil. Number two is the character you're making the documentary about—I think of him as the Primo Levi character—a man who has endured great evil and seems to have emerged from it intact. I think those characters form a rather interesting contrast. One is purely innocent and the other appears to be innocent despite everything and yet surrenders to a mysterious despair.

Right. One is genuinely innocent because she's young. And I always feel young people are innocent. I always feel young people do have a certain beautiful innocence to them that's touching and remarkable to see. The professor was intellectual, and so all his insights and all his philosophy about life, while valid and deep and profound, was . . . was the product of intellectualism, and he had lived too much and, and seen too much. You can intellectualize all the time and you can have ideas about things and discuss things, but finally in your heart there's an empty feeling about existence that no amount of thinking and no amount of conversation and literature and learning ever really fills.

Do those people just snap? Is that what happened to Primo Levi? Is that what happens to this character in the movie?

Well, I don't—they weren't sure. In Primo Levi's case they weren't sure. The question was, did he fall or did he jump? In my character's case, he [definitely] committed suicide. He had many insights into life, but his approach to life . . . it was a good approach, but it was intellectual, and no matter how profound an intellectual you can be, there is a hollowness at your core, a hollowness that cannot be filled by learning and by rational thought. And it got to him finally and he killed himself.

I want to talk about gangsters. There is the gangster in Crimes and Misdemeanors. *There's the gangster in* Bullets over

Broadway. *There are the gangsters in* Broadway Danny Rose. *These kinds of lowlifes at first don't seem to fit in the general world you live in, and yet they're incredible presences, perhaps because they're so outrageous, almost intrusive in this smooth little world of people prattling and chatting. What do those figures represent to you?*

I always was interested in gangsters, and people don't associate me with that because of their image of me on the screen. They think I'm more intellectual than I am, because I wear these glasses and I'm built slightly.

But the truth is I come from the streets of Brooklyn. I'm not educated—I mean, I was thrown out of college in my freshman year. My father was always, you know, a cab driver or a pool hustler. He ran a poolroom. He worked for Albert Anastasia for a while, taking bets at Saratoga. I had always had an interest in and a feeling for that.

I'm not a gangster, but I'm more in that world. I'm more the guy that's home with the beer in his undershirt watching the television set, watching the ball game on television, than I am poring over, you know, the Russian novelists. I mean, I've read these things over the years to keep up with my dates, but the truth of the matter is my heart has always been at the ballpark. So I have a . . . a warm feeling about gangsters. I always like Scorsese's movies, 'cause he always does movies about gangsters, and I always go watch them and enjoy them. That's always a big treat for me when he comes out with a movie.

Are they more in touch with instinct and direct action—and not overintellectualizing things—than other people are?

Well, certainly the gangster in *Bullets over Broadway,* played by Chazz Palminteri, was exactly that for me. I was trying to show in that movie that [someone] who thinks he's the artist, who wants to be the artist, who would hope to be the artist, and has all the, the outer trappings of it [is not necessarily an artist]; that to be an artist is a gift that you're born with, or not born with. John Cusack, in the movie, was not born with it, and he's trying and trying and trying—all from the outside.

Chazz Palminteri, though his life took him in a completely different direction, when push came to shove was truly the creative one of the two, and he was truly the artist. He was the gangster, but he was more in touch with . . . with his soul, or the soul of humanity in some way.

And I thought that was a funny idea, and also a true idea because I truly feel that any artistic gift is a completely born gift, and there's nothing you can learn. I mean, you can learn a few things of craft, a few external things of craft, but the real gift, you're either born with it or you're not. And a gangster was a good person to . . . to make into the real artist, 'cause he was so antithetical [to your expectations]. You know, a gangster is an elemental person, a person who deals with emotions. If he doesn't like the actress in his movie he kills her. There's no debate about it. He doesn't sit and debate the morality of it.

He's . . . he's in touch with his feelings, so to say. So it, it interested me, and I thought it was a funny idea as well.

The other dominant character in Bullets *is Dianne Wiest's actress character. She's fabulous in that movie.*

Dianne dominates with her . . . her acting genius. I've done a few movies with her. She's just a great actress, and you give her anything and she makes it sing. And I gave her this character, and, you know, you turn around and all of a sudden it's like ten times what you've written.

Uh, I'm good that way in that I learned early to hire good people and then take credit for their work.

I suppose Broadway Danny Rose *is among your most unusual movies, isn't it? It's more out of your ordinary country than any other movie. Eric Lax said that Danny Rose was your tribute to Jack Rollins and his loyalty to his people, and that is the characteristic that's wonderful about Danny Rose. He'll die for these terrible acts of his.*

The phenomenon of the personal manager has always interested me in show business, because you always see it, you always see these guys who attach their lives to these actors, and give their lives to these actors, and they do wonderful things for them. And it's a unique occupation, because as [the act] succeeds, you become obsolete. At first the act needs the manager desperately, but as the manager builds the act and, as Jack Rollins would say, nurtures the flower, the act all of a sudden doesn't need the manager anymore. Now the manager is completely unnecessary.

Once you're Jerry Lewis or Frank Sinatra, you don't need the manager. You know, you've got to beat them off with a club is the problem. So it's a very interesting occupation, and I thought it would be a funny one to play. Also, in my limited acting range, the two things I can play are a more intellectual-type guy—I can pass as an intellectual because I have the glasses—and a lowlife, because of the way I am.

I can play a seedy character. I could play a good bookmaker. I could play a Runyonesque character. I could play a gambler or a seedy manager because I've grown up with them, I know them, and I can do it.

So . . . so that's my range. And *Broadway Danny Rose* was an opportunity for me to play that kind of a character that I really can play.

In the middle of that very funny movie you and Mia get into an apartment and you have a whole discussion about life and death and the meaning of both, and all that. Granted it's funny, but it's also surprising—right there at the center of the movie.

Well, that's I guess at the center of my thinking so much. I mean, it's on my mind so much. I guess if we were to socialize, you'd find that I brought that subject up a lot. And it creeps into my movies in joke form. But as you say, [this movie] was in the vernacular. It was a [sudden] comprehension of life, the deeper part of life, as seen by two people who were not intellectuals in any way at all—not literate even.

What about sisters? They're in your movies almost as often as gangsters, these intricate, rather large families with lots of sisters.

Sisters are great because, whether it's two or three, you know, there's always dramatic possibilities. I just feel you have a natural conflict all the time when there's a sibling around. If you look at something as wonderful as *A Streetcar Named Desire,* there are two sisters in the house with the guy. As soon as you get that kind of, of fuel, you can get a fire out of it very, very easily. You see a lot of it in Bergman, and I rely on it a certain amount. It's just a [way] to start conflict.

And the whole notion of certainty. I was thinking really about Mighty Aphrodite, *also* Shadows and Fog. *The guy in* Mighty Aphrodite *could not believe that that girl could produce that wonderful child. In* Shadows and Fog *there's an exchange you and Mia have about certainty—you're looking up at the stars and she's saying, "That star could be dead," and it comes as a shock to your character. The light is coming down, but the star is dead. Is certainty something that you miss and want and can't have?*

Sure. You know, you can never resolve the epistemological conundrum. I once did a joke a long time ago about having to take God's existence on faith, and then I realized that I had to take my own existence on faith. And that really is the truth— that you can't be certain of anything.

I mean, you're in such a precarious position. We're all given this spectacular denial system, and also a mind that puts all this chaos in order. But the truth of the matter is, if you stop and think about it, or lie on your pillow at three o'clock in the morning when you can't sleep and think about it, which is worse, the certainty of everything is very dicey. I mean, you know a lot less than you think you know.

Is that what's going on with that character, the character in Mighty Aphrodite?

Yes, he wants to know. I wanted to make a Greek tragedy—or not a Greek tragedy, but a Greek play—out of it, so that the more he progressed, the more he learned, like Oedipus, the worse off he became, and [you] wanted to shake him and say, "Stop learning so much about—stop trying to investigate so much, 'cause what you're going to learn you're not going to like." Which you could have said to Oedipus and, and you could say to my character in the movie.

The more he learns about and investigates, the worse the facts emerge to him, and then at the end of the movie he's left with total uncertainty. He has her child and she has his child, and they don't know it.

I think the notion in a comedy—and it's also a very realistic modern comedy—of having a Greek chorus, which actually becomes quite a comical entity in itself, that's a great idea. Where did you come up with that?

I just thought that would be a funny thing. I guess one thing that's occurred to me in a general sense over the years, uh, is that a lot of things that are taken for granted as very serious, like the documentary style of filmmaking, or a Greek chorus, can also be used comically and very effectively because of their inherent solemnity. So when that chorus is intoning things, you know, it sounds funny, funnier than one guy saying it.

Of course. Don't be a schmuck, they all say.

Right. It sounds funny when a Greek chorus is saying it, because of the inherent solemnity of the phenomenon.

I don't want this to be painful for you now, but running these pictures so close together, I am struck by how really good Mia Farrow is as an actress.

Mia. Oh, she's wonderful. I always thought she was underrated because she was raised in Hollywood and sort of taken for granted. But I found her to be a terrific actress with a very good range.

An incredible range. I think of her in Broadway Danny Rose, *on the one hand, and* Alice, *on the other hand, as real contrasts. Of all the actresses you've had—and you've had great actresses—she, for you, has had the chance to exhibit a huge range. I think too of* Purple Rose.

Yeah, she did some great work too in *September*. The movie didn't please enough people, so it wasn't seen, but she was quite wonderful in that, which is another aspect of her range. I've been blessed over the years. I've worked with tremendous people, and I don't direct them a lot. I try to speak to them as infrequently as possible, you know. But if you're working with Mia, or Dianne Wiest, or Judy Davis, or Diane Keaton . . . I've worked with Meryl Streep, I've worked with Jody Foster, Tracey Ullman, and Julie Kavner, and I mean you just go on and on, you know—Julia Roberts and, and Téa Leoni and Helen Hunt. I don't speak to them much. Once in a while I have to say something, but not a lot. And they've given these great performances.

And everybody says, "Oh, the direction is so great." "The director is so great." But the truth of the matter is, it's really a minimalist approach. I mean, it's keeping away from them.

Is maybe being a minimalist as far as performance is concerned the secret of being a good director? Maybe just being quiet and watchful and offering a tiny suggestion or something?

Yeah, if you hire good people—if you hire good people and you get out of their way and let them do what has made them great. That's just the way I've always done it. I've gotten great performances over the years out of people. I mean, I haven't gotten the performance out of them. They come and bring them, you know. They've worked out all the notes. And I let them improvise freely. I'm not someone who's, who's dedicated to the script. I mean, I let them change things left and right, improvise, ad-lib, throw things out.

That's interesting. If you were a writer for hire—for some reason they want to be on the set, and if anybody wants to change a comma they want to have their input. I feel the same way about editing. There's a million ways to say any given thought, and if someone else's is as good as mine and they're adamant about it, it's okay with me.

Right, that's what I feel. You know, the guy coming in delivering coffee, if he's got a good idea, if he happens to notice the Avid, and sees that I've edited a scene he's looking at, and he gives me a bad look and says not funny, you know, I have as much faith in his judgment as my own.

I've noticed in looking at your work over the last several weeks that you've become an enormously sophisticated filmmaker, it seems to me. I like the long takes. The camera is almost a character in some sense. That kind of direction builds emotional intensity and brings you, the audience, into a sequence much more profoundly than a sequence with a lot of cuts.

Yeah, I'm not a big cutter. I mean, sometimes you have to cut—if two people are opposite each other in a restaurant or something. But the truth of the matter is, years ago I got onto long takes because I found a lot of reasons to use them, but one great reason is that the actors love them.

I don't do any coverage, so all day I'll be working out the blocking with the cameraman, all day long, for a shot that's maybe seven pages long. And at three o'clock in the afternoon, or four o'clock or something, the actors will do it. And they'll do it a couple of times—I don't shoot a lot of takes—and it's over, and they don't have to do his close-up and her close-up, and back to his close-up and do it again and again and again. They get a chance to do five minutes of material, or seven minutes of material, or three minutes of material, instead of one sentence and cut, and then turn the camera around. I just like that better.

What are some of the other reasons you like it? That's a good reason right there, but you said you have several reasons.

It doesn't jar the audience, you know. You become unaware that it's film. It's there—the camera is there—and a person crosses at the right time, and each person is on film at the right moment, in front of the lens.

That takes a lot of direction on your part.

A lot of blocking, yeah. But not a lot of direction to the actors. Not a lot of motivational conversations and stuff.

You know, I want to say this while your tape is still running, if I can, just get this in, if I can.

We've talked for a while about my films, and I don't want to fall into the category of one of those guys who talks about his films and from his conversation they sound great. But then you see the films, and, you know, there's nothing special. And that could easily happen.

So, I just want to say that I myself am very critical of my films. I feel I've failed almost every time out of the box with my films. There have been very few that I feel are successful, and I don't make any claims for any of them. I'm thankful that people like them at all, but I make no claims when I talk about them. You know, if you've never seen any of them, you might get the idea, "Hey, gee, this sounds like it's interesting and profound and deep, and this film is about something." Then you see the film and you think, "What were they talking about?" So I just want to guard against that.

I'll just put on tape that I think you have made at least a half-dozen of the great movies of the postwar years. So I think you're full of shit about this.

Well, I . . . I . . . as long as long as people know how I feel about them.

It is a wonderful body of work, and I understand where you're coming from—but what are the movies you think are successful?

Well, I, I, um . . .

Not to contradict you, but you said there are a few that you think are okay.

There are, yes, [ones that] are successful for me, in my terms. When I'm home lying on my bed and I'm writing something, I have these incredible ideas. I think I'm going to write *Citizen Kane* every time out of the box, and it's going to be great. And then I make the film, and I'm so humiliated by what I see afterward I think: Where did I go wrong? Was it the editing? Was it my writing? Was I lax in the directing?

So when I finally get a film and I think this film is pretty close to what I was writing at home, I think this is a successful film. Now the audience may hate it. I thought that about *Star-*

dust Memories, and the audience didn't really cotton to it at all. But for me it was a successful film. And there have been a couple like that, where I had an idea, and I brought it off. *Husbands and Wives* was a film like that. I thought I brought that off—that I had an idea and I brought it off.

I'm so glad you brought that up, because with Hollywood Ending *it's one of the two movies I really wanted to get in before we stop. That's an interesting movie in that it's stylistically very different from your other movies. Why did you want to adopt that style for that movie?*

Well, I thought this: I was making a movie about a group of very neurotic people, and I had always wanted to make a movie where I obeyed absolutely none of the niceties of cinema in any way at all. Where I just turned on the lights. Where I shot and began and stopped when I wanted. Where I couldn't care less if people were facing in the right direction. Where I just would jump-cut whenever I wanted. Where I'd just stop and cut and couldn't care less if it was neat. Where I would cut the soundtrack when I wanted. Where I wouldn't mix the film. Where I would just use the [production] track. And I felt that idea would work with these kinds of people and this kind of story, because they were all so emotionally discombobulated and so psychologically dissonant.

You could maybe say these people are sort of half finished, and the movie has a kind of half-finished feel to it.

Yes, exactly. It's not, um, a finely wrought thing. It's supposed to be raw, and they're raw, and, and that's what the film was supposed to be about. And for me that was one of my most successful films.

Was that kind of liberating for you to do?

It was great. And I would like to do that again, because when you work that way, it's a wonderful feeling to know I couldn't care less about any of the so-called rules of cinema. I'm just going to do whatever I want to do and, and I'll be wrong all the time—you know, the exact opposite of what they teach you in a film class.

And yet you don't seem to be a guy who cared particularly for Godard, who's done a lot of that kind of thing.

Well, I like Godard, as an innovator more than the films, although a couple of his films were quite wonderful, just wonderful. But his innovations, I thought, were incredibly imaginative and [maybe] utilized by other people more fruitfully.

And when he asked me to be in a film of his I was so honored, you know, even though it was a little, tiny thing, I was happy to do it for nothing, just 'cause it was him, you know.

I didn't realize you had done that.

No, I did a tiny thing in an awful film he made called *King Lear.*

Oh, right.

And it just . . . I never saw the film, but I could tell when we shot it it was awful.

That brings me somewhat circuitously to the director in Hollywood Ending—*also a gifted, troubled, slightly crazy guy. To me that's a wonderful character, and I think it's a wonderful film.*

It's one of the films I thought was successful for me. It's one of the films I've actually liked that I've made. I liked it 'cause I thought the idea came off. It was fortuitous because I work hard on every film, and yet, as I've said, I don't think they all come off by any means. *Hollywood Ending* I worked hard on, and it worked. Everything fell in. It was just good luck for me.

What about it works for you particularly?

The simplicity of it works for me. I shot it simply. The performances work. The story unfolds correctly. I mean you're going along and the plot developments work all along, and the jokes, I find, are funny enough to engage an intelligent person. They're not silly jokes. They're decent jokes, respectable jokes. And I just thought it worked. I think people will watch that movie and enjoy it. I actually do.

The blind movie director is one of those astonishing ideas. It's just a great idea. Did that just come upon you one day?

Um, no. I can't really give you the provenance of that, but it was something that had come up in a conversation between Marshall Brickman and myself years ago, on a movie we were going to do about an escape artist, a magician. And it just seemed better in this context.

It was going to be a blind escape artist?

Uh, no, he was an escape artist who was having psychological problems—he was having problems getting locked in confined spaces. And one of his psychological problems was that he eventually, psychosomatically lost his sight. And, and then over the years, it metamorphosed into this.

It does have some Woody themes. There is the marriage that wasn't so hot, and she's off with the wrong guy and . . . But also, from your point of view as an actor, it offers opportunities for some of your best physical comedy. I'm thinking in particular of the hotel room scene where you're blind and you have to find your way. . . . That's a really brilliant piece of physical comedy.

Yeah, the idea lent itself very well to comedy. And I felt, in this case, that I didn't blow it, that I don't have the feeling of, "Oh, God, if I could only do this over or that over." I felt that I did it, I got the juice out of the idea. That's always important to me. Now, I hope people like it. If they do, I'll feel delighted. If they don't . . .

You know what people are going to say about it. They'll say that's Woody, he's complaining again about how he's misunderstood as a director, and only the French understand him. It has that potential for the same kind of comments that were visited on Stardust Memories and on Celebrity. It'll seem to cut close to your persona, although you're obviously not blind and obviously not self-important.

Right, but that I can't help. I mean, people are free to, you know, write and interpret these things, or impute to them anything they want. Some people may come up with good insight. Some people may come up with clichés. My feeling is that the simplicity of the idea will be winning to people, that they'll just go in and have a good laugh. Now, I may be wrong. I've been wrong before. There were times when I thought a film was going to do very well for an audience and, uh, and nobody came.

You know, for instance, when I made *Manhattan Murder Mystery* I thought that was a funny murder mystery. And it was fun to make, and I thought it came off. But it didn't have a big audience. And I don't know why. It was completely accessible. To me it was the kind of murder mystery that I had seen when I was growing up, and I thought it was funny, that it was done well. The jokes were good. And the performers did a good job in it. And it was well received, but it just didn't have a big audience.

You said to me last summer that you were going through your drawers and finding some sketchy ideas that you decided to develop, though they're rather lighter-minded than some of your other films. Is that a place where you're at right now?

Well, I was looking at my old ideas and I saw the idea for *Small-time Crooks,* which I thought was a funny idea—they rob a bank, and, you know, the cookie store becomes a success. And I saw the idea for *The Jade Scorpion*—that the hypnotist was actually committing the crimes. That interested me. And this idea for *Hollywood Ending* . . .

And I wanted to do those films 'cause I thought they were all amusing ideas, that I'd have a good time doing them and that people would enjoy the pictures, that they were perfectly respectable pictures. So I've done them. Now what I do next I don't know. I don't know that I would continue in exactly that vein 'cause, you know, those three I wanted to get done so my drawer didn't pile up with comic ideas that, you know, they find after I'm dead.

That little reversal you mention in Small-time Crooks *is kind of familiar from some of your other work, where people are busily going along a path and what happens is the cookie store becomes a surprise success.*

Right. That's my magical background. That's misdirection. That's what I did in *Bullets over Broadway,* where you think one guy's the artist but it turns out to be the other guy. I've done it other places where I lead the audience to believe something, but the movie is really going to be about something else—it really has another twist to it. That's part of the pleasure one gets in performing magic for people too—the technique a magician uses when he's doing a trick, to drop little clues that the audience picks up on, and they go off in that direction, thinking they're on to something, but it's not that. And it works very well when you're doing a comic plot.

Afterword

MISDIRECTION! As Woody's final topic in this interview, it seems to me an appropriate one. His late career seems to me all misdirection. This is all well and good, artistically speaking, but he also has to live in the real world—the commercial world, where movies are marketed to infinitely distracted, often mysteriously misinformed audiences. It is a world where magic is in very short supply.

American movie audiences nowadays like to know, in advance, what they're buying. Is it a romantic comedy? A special-effects extravaganza? A teen-slanted vulgarity? Or, in Academy Award season, something that's supposed to be profound and demanding? Positioning a movie for its appropriate niche is what marketing is all about.

For a long time Woody tried to ignore that. If, as a critic, you went to a screening of one of his films, you were not handed the traditional set of notes as you entered the theater. They were passed out afterward and consisted of cast and credits only. There was no descriptive material designed to "position" the film for you. It was the same with the advertising—no copy lines to give you a clue. It was rather like the openings of his movies. There was never a precredit suggestion—no action-filled or laughter-inducing hint of pleasures to come, no cute animated sequence to get you in a comic mood. There were just these black cards with white writing on them. All the actors, no matter how large their stardom, were listed alphabetically on a single card, with major technical credits on single cards, ending with a simple "Written and Directed by" card for Woody. He has never taken the proprietary ("A Film by . . .") credit. For all you could discern, you were about to see a new version of *The Lower Depths.*

In recent years Woody has relented somewhat on some of these matters. He will at least do a few television interviews (especially in the—for him—prime European market) supporting his releases. Or grant one or two print interviews. But he still does not wish to be caught explaining himself, or trying to cue his audience's response. Artists simply don't do that. As far as he's concerned, they're on their own, free to make what they will of his work—just as readers of what we've learned to call "literary" fiction are.

This lack of pretension reads, to many I think, as a form of pretension. Would it kill him to add a splash of color? Loosen up a little bit? It may even hint at something retro, slightly out of it, in his sensibility. Which is not necessarily wrong.

We are all conditioned by the values of our formative years. And, as our interview makes clear, Woody is no exception. The music he likes best is traditional jazz. The New York he likes best is the New York that dazzled him as a child. The food he eats, the clothes he wears, are not of the latest fashion. Nor are the more abstract issues that preoccupy him. He speaks of Camus, not Derrida. If there's a general theme that he returns to over and over again in his movies, it is trust and its betrayal, the problem of honesty, authenticity in human behavior, particularly when it comes to sex and romance.

These are matters that much concerned those of us who came of age in the immediate postwar years, particularly in the apolitical 1950s, when contempt for Eisenhower, Nixon, and Dulles took the form of withdrawal from the political process that somehow elected them. Woody might eventually appear in a movie about McCarthyism (*The Front* in 1976), but he would not write or direct such a film.

As Adam Gopnik recently observed in *The New Yorker,* Woody came of age in a period when the chief satirical target of sophisticated comedians (Mort Sahl, Nichols and May, even Lenny Bruce) was a certain set of liberal-minded cultural attitudes. As he notes, these comedians, like Woody, rarely took up purely political issues. Indeed, politically speaking the liberals have had tough sledding for decades—only quasiliberals (like shifty Bill Clinton) needed to apply for admission to the White House. But culturally—it's what has made neoconservatives crazy for years—they have achieved dominance. On everything from Mahler's symphonies to recreational marijuana to sexual morality, they have won the cultural wars. But I think this crowd, at once Woody's prime targets and natural audience, have grown less willing to laugh at themselves as they've grown older. Worse, with moronic conservatism—oh, pardon me, "compassionate" conservatism—

dominant in national politics and liberalism in wimpish disarray, it is even harder for Woody to get them laughing. Somehow, in its presently embattled state, it seems disloyal to larger
liberal principles to have fun with—or, for that matter, to take
seriously—romantic infidelity. Not when *Roe v. Wade* is
within one vote of being overturned by the Supreme Court.
Woody makes an excellent moose joke in *Hollywood Ending.*
But . . . the caribou are a species endangered by drilling for oil
in Alaska.

The tyranny of the self-righteous was so much easier to
make fun of—so much less dangerous—when smiling Eisenhower was in the White House and his favorite preacher was
not some racist right-wing crazy but the relatively benign—
and genially profit-oriented—Norman Vincent Peale.

Our generation, mine and Woody's, does, I think, seem
sort of old-fashioned. We can sympathize with, say, feminism,
make the right noises when environmental issues arise, we can
even catch the tone of modern talk—use its slang and catch-
phrases appropriately in our "discourse," for instance—but
our audience sniffs out, alas, the lack of hipness in our hearts.

This failure, if failure it be, does not weigh heavily on our
hearts. We know, to borrow a phrase, that "it's still the same
old story, a fight for love and glory . . . as time goes by." Our
direct connection to modernism, whether it is expressed in the
stylizations of *Shadows and Fog,* or the Freudian underpin-
nings of something like *Husbands and Wives,* or our horror at
the demise of God (*Crimes and Misdemeanors*), does not seem
old-fashioned to us. We think these questions are eternal and

worthy of our serious attention. Camus may be out of fashion, but the issues he raised will never go away.

But, to return to the practical world, Woody's stubbornness in raising these matters, in the particular terms he does, is a significant factor in making him nowadays a marketing nightmare. I have known one or two people who have tried to push him toward a more pro-active stance when they are trying to sell one of his pictures. These are not necessarily crass or materialistic individuals. They like his pictures, they like Woody, they sincerely want to help him find a bigger audience. But to no—or no better than minimal—avail.

But set aside, for the moment, Woody's own austerity when it comes to the marketplace. Let's return, instead, to "misdirection." Essentially, with Woody, you are selling comedy. It is the only broad generic category into which the majority of his movies can be made to fit. He knows that, the marketers know it, the critics know it, and so does the audience. But, well and richly gagged though many of them are, you would not call any of them—at least since *Annie Hall*—laff riots. *Zelig* and *The Purple Rose of Cairo* and *Bullets over Broadway* and, yes, *Celebrity* are profoundly funny movies, rich in irony and social satire. Even *Hollywood Ending* is, among other things, a very sharp satire on *auteur*ship, a formerly high critical concept which is now a commonplace.

But these pictures are not *Ace Ventura, Pet Detective,* which is an exercise in pop postmodernism. Nor are they *Sleepless in Seattle,* which is an exercise in genteel nostalgia, without an idea in its pretty, empty little head. Woody's movies are not pictures you can presell—or help the audience predigest—with a line or two of advertising copy. Or a quick-cut trailer. The pleasures they offer are complicated ones, at least by the standards of our crude and witless times. In a sense they represent (and I hate to say this) failed attempts at misdirection on Woody's part. He'd like us to believe they are comedies. And, indeed, by his standards (and mine) they are funny. But not in any easily salable way.

So, to put the matter bluntly, he's screwed—at least as far as his native land is concerned. To resort to an old term of art in the advertising game, he has no "Unique Selling Proposition," no simple concept that sends audiences into the theater in a confidently expectant mood and then sends them out, after the show, with their expectations happily satisfied. This man is nothing but trouble.

Except, of course, to the Europeans, always distant and top-lofty about American life, who still feel free to laugh at the desperate scurryings recorded in films like *Husbands and Wives* or *Deconstructing Harry*. I'm of course with them. I basically despise the quality of modern American life—its history-free culture, its pietistic politics, the grinding stupidity of our public discourse on every topic. I suspect Woody feels the same but is too smart to say so openly.

It is one reason why misdirection and magic loom so large in his work. It is the improbable—no, totally impossible—intervention he devoutly wishes for. And knows can never happen. We must leave him there, in his wistfulness. With death looming ever nearer. But with his brass balls still intact, still clanging.

He will never change. Maybe we will—circle back on him, pick up on him again. Or maybe, despite his dubiety, posterity will see him for what he has been—a great and serious comic artist, telling the truth—well, anyway, some significant truths—about his time and his place and, yes, about certain ineluctable aspects of—forgive the pompous phrase— "the human condition." That, obviously, is where my bet is placed.

Filmography

Note: This filmography includes only those films written and/or directed by Woody Allen. It lists only principal players and the major technical contributors to his movies.

What's New, Pussycat (1965)

Directed by Clive Donner
Written by Woody Allen

Cast:

Peter Sellers....	Dr. Fritz Fassbender
Peter O'Toole....	Michael James
Romy Schneider....	Carole Werner
Capucine....	Renee Lefebvre
Paula Prentiss....	Liz Bien
Woody Allen....	Victor Skakapopulis
Ursula Andress....	Rita

Produced by Charles K. Feldman
Executive Producer, John C. Shepridge
Producer, Richard Sylbert
Original Music by Burt Bacharach
Lyrics by Hal David
Arranged and Conducted by Charles Blackwell
Songs Performed by Tom Jones, Dionne Warwick
Director of Photography, Jean Badal
Film Editor, Fergus McDonell
Production Design, Jacques Saulnier

Art Direction, Jacques Saulnier
Costume Design, Mia Fonssagrives
Title Design by Richard Williams
Running time: 108 min

What's Up, Tiger Lily? (1966)

Directed by Woody Allen, Senkichi Taniguchi
Writing credits (in alphabetical order):
Woody Allen
Julie Bennett
Frank Buxton
Louise Lasser
Len Maxwell
Mickey Rose
Bryan Wilson

Cast:

Tatsuya Mihashi....	Interpol Agent/Phil Moscowitz
Akiko Wakabayashi....	Mystery Moll #1/Suki Yaki
Mie Hama....	Mystery Moll #2/Teri Yaki
Tadao Nakamaru....	Drug-running Gangster/Shepherd Wong
Susumu Kurobe....	Smiling Gangster/Wing Fat
Woody Allen....	Narrator/Voice of Phil Moscowitz

Produced by Woody Allen
Original Music by Jack Lewis, The Lovin' Spoonful
Cinematography by Kazuo Yamada
Film Editing by Richard Krown
Running time: 80 min

Take the Money and Run (1969)

Directed by Woody Allen
Written by Woody Allen, Mickey Rose

Cast:

Woody Allen....	Virgil Starkwell
Janet Margolin....	Louise
Lonny Chapman....	Jake
James Anderson....	Chain Gang Warden
Jackson Beck....	Narrator
Louise Lasser....	Kay Lewis

Executive Producer, Sidney Glazier
Associate Producer, Jack Grossberg
Produced by Charles H. Joffe, Jack Rollins
Original Music by Marvin Hamlisch
Director of Photography, Lester Shorr

Film Editors, Paul Jordan, Ron Kalish
Casting, Marvin Paige
Art Director, Fred Harpman
Set Decoration, Marvin March
Production Managers, Fred T. Gallo, Jack Grossberg
Assistant Directors, Walter Hill, Louis A. Stroller
Special Effects, A. D. Flowers
Running time: 85 min

Bananas (1971)

Directed by Woody Allen
Written by Woody Allen, Mickey Rose

Cast:

Woody Allen....	Fielding Mellish
Louise Lasser....	Nancy
Carlos Montalbán....	General Emilio M. Vargas
Natividad Abascal....	Yolanda
Jacobo Morales....	Esposito
Miguel Suárez....	Luis
David Ortiz....	Sanchez
René Enríquez....	Diaz
Jack Axelrod....	Arroyo
Howard Cosell....	Himself
Roger Grimsby....	Himself
Don Dunphy....	Himself
Charlotte Rae....	Mrs. Mellish
Stanley Ackerman....	Dr. Mellish

Produced by Axel Anderson, Antonio Encarnacion, Jack Grossberg
Executive Producer, Charles H. Joffe
Associate Producer, Ralph Rosenblum
Producer, Manolon Villamil
Original Music by Marvin Hamlisch
Cinematography by Andrew M. Costikyan
Film Editors, Ron Kalish, Ralph Rosenblum
Casting, Vicky Hernández
Production Design, Ed Wittstein
Set Decoration, Herbert F. Mulligan
Costume Design, Gene Coffin
Production Manager, Morton Gorowitz
Assistant Director, Fred T. Gallo
Special Effects, Don B. Courtney
Running time: 82 min

Play It Again, Sam (1972)

Directed by Herbert Ross
Written by Woody Allen, based on his play

Cast:
Woody Allen....	Allan
Diane Keaton....	Linda
Tony Roberts....	Dick
Jerry Lacy....	Bogart
Susan Anspach....	Nancy
Jennifer Salt....	Sharon
Joy Bang....	Julie
Viva....	Jennifer

Executive Producer, Charles H. Joffe
Produced by Arthur P. Jacobs
Associate Producer, Frank Capra, Jr.
Original Music, Billy Goldenberg, Oscar Peterson ("Blues for Allan Felix")
Music from "Casablanca" by Max Steiner, Herman Hupfeld ("As Time Goes By")
Director of Photography, Owen Roizman
Film Editor, Marion Rothman
Production Design, Ed Wittstein
Set Decoration, Doug von Koss
Costume Design, Anna Hill Johnstone
Production Supervisor, Roger M. Rothstein
Assistant Director, William Gerrity
Running time: 85 min

Everything You Always Wanted to Know About Sex (1972)

Directed by Woody Allen
Written by Woody Allen
Based on the book by David Reuben

Cast:
Woody Allen....	The Fool/Fabrizio/Victor Shakapopulis/Sperm #1
John Carradine....	Dr. Bernardo
Lou Jacobi....	Sam
Louise Lasser....	Gina
Anthony Quayle....	The King
Tony Randall....	The Operator
Lynn Redgrave....	The Queen
Burt Reynolds....	Sperm Switchboard Chief
Gene Wilder....	Dr. Doug Ross
Jack Barry....	Himself
Erin Fleming....	The Girl
Elaine Giftos....	Dr. Ross
Toni Holt....	Herself
Robert Q. Lewis....	Himself

Heather MacRae....   Helen Lacey
Pamela Mason....   Herself
Sidney Miller....   George
Regis Philbin....   Himself
Alan Caillou....   The Fool's Father
Geoffrey Holder....   Sorcerer
Jay Robinson....   The Priest
Ref Sanchez....   Igor
Baruch Lumet....   Rabbi Chaim Baumel

Executive Producer, Jack Brodsky
Produced by Charles H. Joffe
Associate Producer, Jack Grossberg
Original Music Composed and Conducted by Mundell Lowe
Director of Photography, David M. Walsh
Film Editor, Eric Albertson
Casting, Marvin Paige
Production Design, Dale Hennesy
Set Decoration, Marvin March
Assistant Director, Fred T. Gallo, Terry M. Carr (second)
Visual Effects, Harvey Plastrik
Running time: 87 min

Sleeper (1973)

Directed by Woody Allen
Written by Woody Allen, Marshall Brickman

Cast:
Woody Allen....   Miles Monroe
Diane Keaton....   Luna Schlosser
John Beck....   Erno Windt
Mary Gregory....   Dr. Melik
Don Keefer....   Dr. Tryon
John McLiam....   Dr. Aragon
Bartlett Robinson....   Dr. Orva
Chris Forbes....   Rainer Krebs
Marya Small....   Dr. Nero
Peter Hobbs....   Dr. Dean

Produced by Marshall Brickman, Jack Grossberg
Associate Producer, Ralph Rosenblum
Executive Producer, Charles H. Joffe
Original Music, Woody Allen
Director of Photography, David M. Walsh
Film Editors, O. Nicholas Brown, Ron Kalish, Ralph Rosenblum
Casting, Lynn Stalmaster
Production Design, Dale Hennesy
Set Decoration, Gary Moreno
Costume Design, Joel Schumacher

Assistant Director, Fred T. Gallo, Henry J. Lange Jr. (second)
Special Effects, A. D. Flowers
Visual Effects, Harvey Plastrik
Stunt Coordinator, M. James Arnett
Running time: 89 min

Love and Death (1975)

Directed by Woody Allen
Written by Woody Allen

Cast:

Woody Allen....	Boris Grushenko
Diane Keaton....	Sonja
Georges Adet....	Old Nehamkin
Frank Adu....	Drill sergeant
Edward Ardisson....	Priest
Féodor Atkine....	Mikhail Grushenko
Yves Barsacq....	Rimsky
Olga Georges-Picot....	Countess Alexandrovna
Harold Gould....	Anton Inbedkov
Harry Hankin....	Uncle Sasha
Jessica Harper....	Natasha
C. A. R. Smith....	Father Nikolai
James Tolkan....	Napoleon Bonaparte

Executive Producer, Martin Poll
Produced by Charles H. Joffe, Jack Rollins
Associate Producer, Fred T. Gallo
Music, Sergei Prokofiev
Director of Photography, Ghislain Cloquet
Film Editors, Ron Kalish, Ralph Rosenblum
Casting, Miriam Brickman, Juliet Taylor, Blanche Wiesenfeld
Production Design, Will Holt
Costume Design, Gladys de Segonzac
Unit Manager, Jean-Marie Durand
Assistant Director, Bernard Cohn, Paul Feyder (second)
Special Effects, Kit West
Stunts, Gábor Piroch
Running time: 85 min

Annie Hall (1977)

Directed by Woody Allen
Written by Woody Allen, Marshall Brickman

Cast:

Woody Allen....	Alvy Singer
Diane Keaton....	Annie Hall

Tony Roberts....   Rob
Carol Kane....   Allison Portchnik
Paul Simon....   Tony Lacey
Shelley Duvall....   Pam
Janet Margolin....   Robin
Colleen Dewhurst....   Annie's Mom
Christopher Walken.... Duane Hall
Donald Symington....   Annie's Dad
Helen Ludlam....   Grammy Hall

Executive Producer, Robert Greenhut
Produced by Charles H. Joffe, Jack Rollins
Associate Producer, Fred T. Gallo
Director of Photography, Gordon Willis
Film Editors, Wendy Greene Bricmont, Ralph Rosenblum
Casting, Juliet Taylor
Art Direction, Mel Bourne
Set Decoration, Robert Drumheller, Justin Scoppa, Jr.
Costume Design, Ralph Lauren, Ruth Morley
Production Manager, Robert Greenhut
Assistant Director, Fred T. Gallo, Fred Blankfein (second)
Running time: 93 min

Interiors (1978)

Directed by Woody Allen
Written by Woody Allen

Cast:
Kristin Griffith....   Flyn
Mary Beth Hurt....   Joey
Richard Jordan....   Frederick
Diane Keaton....   Renata
E. G. Marshall....   Arthur
Geraldine Page....   Eve
Maureen Stapleton....   Pearl
Sam Waterston....   Mike

Executive Producer, Robert Greenhut
Produced by Charles H. Joffe, Jack Rollins
Director of Photography, Gordon Willis
Film Editor, Ralph Rosenblum
Casting, Juliet Taylor
Production Design, Mel Bourne
Set Decoration, Mario Mazzola, Daniel Robert
Costume Design, Joel Schumacher
Production Manager, John Nicolella
Assistant Director, Martin Berman
Running time: 93 min

Manhattan (1979)

Directed by Woody Allen
Written by Woody Allen, Marshall Brickman

Cast:

Woody Allen....	Isaac Davis
Diane Keaton....	Mary Wilkie
Michael Murphy....	Yale
Mariel Hemingway....	Tracy
Meryl Streep....	Jill
Anne Byrne....	Emily
Karen Ludwig....	Connie
Michael O'Donoghue....	Dennis
Wallace Shawn....	Jeremiah

Executive Producers, Robert Greenhut, Charles H. Joffe, Jack Rollins
Music by George Gershwin
Conducted by Zubin Mehta
Director of Photography, Gordon Willis
Film Editor, Susan E. Morse
Casting, Juliet Taylor
Production Design, Mel Bourne
Set Decoration, Robert Drumheller
Costume Design, Albert Wolsky
Production Manager, Martin Danzig
Assistant Director, Frederic B. Blankfein, Joan Spiegel Feinstein (second)
Running time: 96 min

Stardust Memories (1980)

Directed by Woody Allen
Written by Woody Allen

Cast:

Woody Allen....	Sandy Bates
Charlotte Rampling....	Dorrie
Jessica Harper....	Daisy
Marie-Christine Barrault....	Isobel

Produced by Robert Greenhut
Executive Producers, Charles H. Joffe, Jack Rollins
Original Music, Dick Hyman
Director of Photography, Gordon Willis
Film Editor, Susan E. Morse
Casting, Juliet Taylor
Production Design, Mel Bourne
Art Direction, Michael Molly
Set Decoration, Steven Jordan
Costume Design, Santo Loquasto
Production Manager, Michael Peyser

Unit Managers, Ezra Swerdlow, Charles Zalben
Assistant Director, Fredric B. Blankfein, Yudi Bennett (second),
   Ed Levy (second)
Running time: 91 min

A Midsummer Night's Sex Comedy (1982)

Directed by Woody Allen
Written by Woody Allen

Cast:

Woody Allen....	Andrew
Mia Farrow....	Ariel
José Ferrer....	Leopold
Julie Hagerty....	Dulcy
Tony Roberts....	Maxwell
Mary Steenburgen....	Adrian

Produced by Robert Greenhut
Executive Producers, Charles H. Joffe, Jack Rollins
Associate Producer, Michael Peyser
Music by Felix Mendelssohn, Robert Schumann
Director of Photography, Gordon Willis
Film Editor, Susan E. Morse
Casting, Juliet Taylor
Production Design, Mel Bourne
Art Direction, Speed Hopkins
Set Decoration, Carol Joffe
Costume Design, Santo Loquasto
Assistant Director, Frederic B. Blankfein, Anthony Gittleson (second),
   Thomas Reilly (second)
Running time: 88 min

Zelig (1983)

Directed by Woody Allen
Written by Woody Allen

Cast:

Woody Allen....	Leonard Zelig
Mia Farrow....	Dr. Eudora Fletcher

Produced by Robert Greenhut
Executive Producers, Charles H. Joffe, Jack Rollins
Associate Producer, Michael Peyser
Original Music, Dick Hyman
Director of Photography, Gordon Willis
Film Editor, Susan E. Morse
Casting, Juliet Taylor

Production Design, Mel Bourne
Art Direction, Speed Hopkins
Set Decoration, Les Bloom, Janet Rosenbloom
Costume Design, Santo Loquasto
Production Manager, Michael Peyser
Unit Manager, Ezra Swerdlow
Assistant Director, Frederic B. Blankfein, James Chory (second),
   Tony Gittleson (second)
Stunts, Pam Barber, Cole Palen
Running time: 79 min

Broadway Danny Rose (1984)

Directed by Woody Allen
Written by Woody Allen

Cast:

Woody Allen....	Danny Rose
Mia Farrow....	Tina Vitale
Nick Apollo Forte....	Lou Canova
Sandy Baron....	Himself
Corbett Monica....	Himself
Jackie Gayle....	Himself
Morty Gunty....	Himself
Will Jordan....	Himself
Howard Storm....	Himself
Jack Rollins....	Himself
Milton Berle....	Himself

Produced by Charles H. Joffe
Associate Producer, Michael Peyser
Original Music, Nick Apollo Forte ("Agita," "My Bambina")
Director of Photography, Gordon Willis
Film Editor, Susan E. Morse
Casting, Juliet Taylor
Production Design, Mel Bourne
Set Decoration, Les Bloom
Costume Design, Jeffrey Kurland
Production Manager, Fredric B. Blankfein
Unit Production Manager, Ezra Swerdlow
Assistant Director, Thomas Reilly, James Chory (second)
Music Supervisor, Dick Hyman
Running time: 84 min

The Purple Rose of Cairo (1985)

Directed by Woody Allen
Written by Woody Allen

Cast:

Mia Farrow....	Cecilia
Jeff Daniels....	Tom Baxter, Gil Shepherd
Danny Aiello....	Monk
Irving Metzman....	Theater Manager
Stephanie Farrow....	Cecilia's Sister
David Kieserman....	Diner Boss
Edward Herrmann....	Henry
John Wood....	Jason
Deborah Rush....	Rita
Van Johnson....	Larry
Zoe Caldwell....	The Countess
Eugene Anthony....	Arturo
Karen Akers....	Kitty Haynes
Annie Joe Edwards....	Delilah
Milo O'Shea....	Father Donnelly
Dianne Wiest....	Emma

Produced by Robert Greenhut
Executive Producers, Charles H. Joffe, Jack Rollins
Associate Producers, Michael Peyser, Gail Sicilia
Original Music, Dick Hyman
Director of Photography, Gordon Willis
Film Editor, Susan E. Morse
Casting, Juliet Taylor
Production Design, Stuart Wurtzel
Art Direction, Edward Pisoni
Set Decoration, Carol Joffe
Costume Design, Jeffrey Kurland
Production Manager, Michael Peyser
Assistant Director, Thomas Reilly, James Chory (second)
Running time: 84 min

Hannah and Her Sisters (1986)

Directed by Woody Allen
Written by Woody Allen

Cast:

Barbara Hershey....	Lee
Carrie Fisher....	April
Michael Caine....	Elliot
Mia Farrow....	Hannah
Dianne Wiest....	Holly
Maureen O'Sullivan....	Norma

Lloyd Nolan....	Evan
Max von Sydow....	Frederick
Woody Allen....	Mickey Sachs
Sam Waterston....	David Tolchin
Daniel Stern....	Dusty
Julie Kavner....	Gail
Joanna Gleason....	Carol
Bobby Short....	Himself
Lewis Black....	Paul
Julia Louis-Dreyfus....	Mary
Christian Clemenson....	Larry
J. T. Walsh....	Ed Smythe
John Turturro....	Writer

Produced by Robert Greenhut
Executive Producers, Charles H. Joffe, Jack Rollins
Associate Producer, Gail Sicilia
Music:
  Johann Sebastian Bach
  James V. Monaco ("You Made Me Love You")
  Giacomo Puccini ("Sola perduta, abbandonata" from *Manon Lescaut*; overture
    from *Madama Butterfly*)
Cinematography, Carlo Di Palma
Film Editor, Susan E. Morse
Casting, Juliet Taylor
Production Design, Stuart Wurtzel
Set Decoration, Carol Joffe
Costume Design, Jeffrey Kurland
Production Manager, Ezra Swerdlow
Assistant Director, Thomas Reilly, Ken Ornstein (second)
Running time: 103 min

Radio Days (1987)

Directed by Woody Allen
Written by Woody Allen

Cast:

Julie Kavner....	Mother
Julie Kurnitz....	Irene
David Warrilow....	Roger
Wallace Shawn....	Masked Avenger
Michael Tucker....	Father
Josh Mostel....	Abe
Renée Lippin....	Aunt Ceil
William Magerman....	Grandpa
Leah Carrey....	Grandma
Joy Newman....	Ruthie
Hy Anzell....	Mr. Waldbaum

Judith Malina....	Mrs. Waldbaum
Dianne Wiest....	Bea
Kenneth Mars....	Rabbi Baumel
Mia Farrow....	Sally White
Larry David....	Communist Neighbor
Rebecca Schaeffer....	Communist's Daughter
Belle Berger....	Mrs. Silverman
Guy Le Bow....	Bull Kern
Brian Mannain....	Kirby Kyle
Stan Burns....	Ventriloquist (as Stan Burns)
Todd Field....	Crooner
Danny Aiello....	Rocco
Gina DeAngelis....	Rocco's Mother
Dwight Weist....	Pearl Harbor Announcer
Jeff Daniels....	Biff Baxter
Kitty Carlisle Hart....	Radio Singer
Tony Roberts....	'Silver Dollar' Emcee
Ivan Kronenfeld....	On-the-spot Newsman
Yolanda Childress....	Polly's Mother
Diane Keaton....	New Year's Singer
Woody Allen....	Narrator

Produced by Robert Greenhut
Executive Producers, Charles H. Joffe, Jack Rollins
Associate Producers, Gail Sicilia, Ezra Swerdlow
Music, Jimmy Eaton ("I Double Dare You"), Edward Eliscu ("The Carioca")
Music Supervisor, Dick Hyman
Director of Photography, Carlo Di Palma
Film Editor, Susan E. Morse
Casting, Juliet Taylor
Production Design, Santo Loquasto
Art Direction, Speed Hopkins
Set Decoration, Les Bloom, Carol Joffe
Costume Design, Jeffrey Kurland
Production Manager, Thomas Reilly
Assistant Director, Ezra Swerdlow, Ken Ornstein (second)
Running time: 85 min

September (1987)

Directed by Woody Allen
Written by Woody Allen

Cast:

Denholm Elliott....	Howard
Dianne Wiest....	Stephanie
Mia Farrow....	Lane
Elaine Stritch....	Diane
Sam Waterston....	Peter

Jack Warden....   Lloyd
Ira Wheeler....   Mr. Raines
Jane Cecil....   Mrs. Raines
Rosemary Murphy....   Mrs. Mason

Produced by Robert Greenhut
Executive Producers, Charles H. Joffe, Jack Rollins
Associate Producer, Gail Sicilia
Director of Photography, Carlo Di Palma
Film Editor, Susan E. Morse
Casting, Juliet Taylor
Production Design, Santo Loquasto
Art Direction, Speed Hopkins
Set Decoration, George DeTitta, Jr.
Costume Design, Jeffrey Kurland
Production Manager, Joseph Hartwick
Assistant Director, Thomas Reilly, Ken Ornstein (second)
Running time: 82 min

Another Woman (1988)

Directed by Woody Allen
Written by Woody Allen

Cast:
Gena Rowlands....   Marion
Mia Farrow....   Hope
Ian Holm....   Ken
Blythe Danner....   Lydia
Gene Hackman....   Larry Lewis
Betty Buckley....   Kathy
Martha Plimpton....   Laura
John Houseman....   Marion's Father
Sandy Dennis....   Claire
David Ogden Stiers....   Young Marion's Father
Philip Bosco....   Sam
Harris Yulin....   Paul
Frances Conroy....   Lynn

Produced by Robert Greenhut
Executive Producers, Charles H. Joffe, Jack Rollins
Associate Producers, Thomas Reilly, Helen Robin
Music:
    Johann Sebastian Bach ("Unaccompanied Cello Suite in D Major," "Sonata for Cello and Piano No. 2, BMV 1028")
    Jerome Kern ("A Fine Romance," "Make Believe")
    Gustav Mahler (*Symphony No. 4*)
    Cole Porter ("You'd Be So Nice to Come Home To")
    Erik Satie ("Movement 3" from *Trois Gymnopédies*, Debussy version)
    Edgard Varèse ("Ecuatorial")

Kurt Weill ("The Bilbao Song")
Director of Photography, Sven Nykvist
Film Editor, Susan E. Morse
Casting, Juliet Taylor
Production Design, Santo Loquasto
Art Direction, Speed Hopkins
Set Decoration, George DeTitta, Jr.
Costume Design, Jeffrey Kurland
Production Manager, Joseph Hartwick
Assistant Director, Thomas A. Reilly, Ken Ornstein (second)
Running time: 84 min

New York Stories ("Oedipus Wrecks" Segment) (1989)

Directed by Woody Allen
Written by Woody Allen

Cast:

Woody Allen....	Sheldon
Marvin Chatinover....	Psychiatrist
Mae Questel....	Mother
Mia Farrow....	Lisa
Julie Kavner....	Treva

Produced by Robert Greenhut
Executive Producers, Charles H. Joffe, Jack Rollins (II)
Director of Photography, Sven Nykvist
Film Editor, Susan E. Morse
Casting, Juliet Taylor
Production Design, Santo Loquasto
Art Direction, Speed Hopkins
Set Decoration, Susan Bode
Costume Design, Jeffrey Kurland
Production Manager, Joseph Hartwick
Assistant Director, Thomas Reilly, Judy Ferguson (second)
Visual Effects, Nancy Bernstein, Joel Hynek, Stuart Robertson, Joseph Iannuzzi
Running time: 119 min (total film)

Crimes and Misdemeanors (1989)

Directed by Woody Allen
Written by Woody Allen

Cast:

Martin Landau....	Judah Rosenthal
Claire Bloom....	Miriam Rosenthal
Anjelica Huston....	Dolores Paley
Woody Allen....	Cliff Stern

Jenny Nichols....	Jenny
Joanna Gleason....	Wendy Stern
Alan Alda....	Lester
Sam Waterston....	Ben
Mia Farrow....	Halley Reed
Martin S. Bergmann....	Prof. Louis Levy
Jerry Orbach....	Jack Rosenthal

Produced by Robert Greenhut
Executive Producers, Charles H. Joffe, Jack Rollins
Associate Producers, Thomas Reilly, Helen Robin
Director of Photography, Sven Nykvist
Film Editor, Susan E. Morse
Casting, Juliet Taylor
Production Design, Santo Loquasto
Art Direction, Speed Hopkins
Set Decoration, Susan Bode
Costume Design, Jeffrey Kurland
Production Manager, Joseph Hartwick
Assistant Director, Thomas Reilly, Richard Patrick (second)
Running time: 107 min

Alice (1990)

Directed by Woody Allen
Written by Woody Allen

Cast:

Mia Farrow....	Alice
Joe Mantegna....	Joe
William Hurt....	Doug
Julie Kavner....	Decorator
Holland Taylor....	Helen
Keye Luke....	Dr. Yang
Judy Davis....	Vicki
Cybill Shepherd....	Nancy Brill
Alec Baldwin....	Ed
Blythe Danner....	Dorothy
Gwen Verdon....	Alice's Mother
Patrick O'Neal....	Alice's Father
Bernadette Peters....	Muse
Elle Macpherson....	Model

Produced by Robert Greenhut
Executive Producers, Charles H. Joffe, Jack Rollins
Co-producers, Joseph Hartwick, Helen Robin
Associate Producers, Jane Read Martin, Thomas Reilly
Director of Photography, Carlo Di Palma
Film Editor, Susan E. Morse
Casting, Juliet Taylor

Production Design, Santo Loquasto
Art Direction, Speed Hopkins
Set Decoration, Susan Bode
Costume Design, Jeffrey Kurland
Production Manager, Joseph Hartwick
Assistant Director, Thomas Reilly
Visual Effects Supervisor, Randall Balsmeyer
Running time: 102 min

Shadows and Fog (1992)

Directed by Woody Allen
Written by Woody Allen

Cast:

Woody Allen....	Max Kleinman
Mia Farrow....	Irmy
John Malkovich....	Clown
Madonna....	Marie
Donald Pleasence....	Doctor
Lily Tomlin....	Prostitute
Jodie Foster....	Prostitute
Kathy Bates....	Prostitute
Anne Lange....	Prostitute
John Cusack....	Student Jack
Kate Nelligan....	Eve
Philip Bosco....	Mr. Paulsen
Julie Kavner....	Alma
Wallace Shawn....	Simon Carr
Kenneth Mars....	Magician
Josef Sommer....	Priest
David Ogden Stiers....	Hacker
Camille Saviola....	Landlady
Tim Loomis....	Dwarf
Katy Dierlam....	Fat Lady
Dennis Vestunis....	Strongman
Michael Kirby....	Killer

Produced by Robert Greenhut
Executive Producers, Charles H. Joffe, Jack Rollins
Co-producers, Joseph Hartwick, Helen Robin
Associate Producer, Thomas Reilly
Music, Kurt Weill (from "Die Dreigroschenoper")
Director of Photography, Carlo Di Palma
Film Editor, Susan E. Morse
Casting, Juliet Taylor
Production Design, Santo Loquasto
Art Direction, Speed Hopkins
Set Decoration, George DeTitta, Jr., Amy Marshall

Costume Design, Jeffrey Kurland
Production Manager, Joseph Hartwick
Assistant Director, Thomas Reilly, Richard Patrick (second)
Visual Effects Supervisor, Randall Balsmeyer
Running time: 85 min

Husbands and Wives (1992)

Directed by Woody Allen
Written by Woody Allen

Cast:

Woody Allen....	Gabe Roth
Mia Farrow....	Judy Roth
Sydney Pollack....	Jack
Judy Davis....	Sally
Juliette Lewis....	Rain
Liam Neeson....	Michael
Ron Rifkin....	Rain's analyst
Blythe Danner....	Rain's mother
Brian McConnachie....	Rain's father

Produced by Robert Greenhut
Executive Producers, Charles H. Joffe, Jack Rollins
Associate Producer, Thomas Reilly
Co-producers, Joseph Hartwick, Helen Robin
Director of Photography, Carlo Di Palma
Film Editor, Susan E. Morse
Casting, Juliet Taylor
Production Design, Santo Loquasto
Art Direction, Speed Hopkins
Set Decoration, Susan Bode
Costume Design, Jeffrey Kurland
Production Manager, Joseph Hartwick
Assistant Director, Thomas Reilly, Richard Patrick (second)
Running time: 108 min

Manhattan Murder Mystery (1993)

Directed by Woody Allen
Written by Woody Allen, Marshall Brickman

Cast:

Woody Allen....	Larry Lipton
Diane Keaton....	Carol Lipton
Jerry Adler....	Paul House
Lynn Cohen....	Lillian House
Ron Rifkin....	Sy
Joy Behar....	Marilyn

William Addy....   Jack, the Super
Alan Alda....   Ted
Anjelica Huston....   Marcia Fox

Produced by Robert Greenhut
Executive Producers, Charles H. Joffe, Jack Rollins
Co-producers, Joseph Hartwick, Helen Robin
Associate Producer, Thomas Reilly
Director of Photography, Carlo Di Palma
Film Editor, Susan E. Morse
Casting, Juliet Taylor
Production Design, Santo Loquasto
Art Direction, Speed Hopkins
Set Decoration, Susan Bode
Costume Design, Jeffrey Kurland
Production Manager, Joseph Hartwick
Assistant Director, Thomas Reilly, Richard Patrick (second)
Running time: 104 min

Bullets Over Broadway (1994)

Directed by Woody Allen
Written by Woody Allen, Douglas McGrath

Cast:
John Cusack....   David Shayne
Jack Warden....   Julian Marx
Dianne Wiest....   Helen Sinclair
Tony Sirico....   Rocco
Jennifer Tilly....   Olive Neal
Rob Reiner....   Sheldon Flender
Chazz Palminteri....   Cheech
Peter Castellotti....   Waterfront Hood (as Pete Castellotti)
Mary-Louise Parker....   Ellen
Harvey Fierstein....   Sid Loomis
Nina Peterson....   Josette (as Nina Sonya Peterson)
Edie Falco....   Lorna
Jim Broadbent....   Warner Purcell
Tracey Ullman....   Eden Brent

Produced by Robert Greenhut
Executive Producers, J. E. Beaucaire, Jean Doumanian
Co-executive Producers, Letty Aronson, Charles H. Joffe, Jack Rollins
Associate Producer, Thomas Reilly
Co-producer, Helen Robin
Director of Photography, Carlo Di Palma
Film Editor, Susan E. Morse
Casting, Juliet Taylor
Production Design, Santo Loquasto
Art Direction, Tom Warren

Set Decoration, Susan Bode, Amy Marshall
Costume Design, Jeffrey Kurland
Production Managers, Jonathan Filley, Helen Robin
Assistant Director, Thomas Reilly, Richard Patrick (second)
Running time: 98 min

Don't Drink the Water (television) (1994)

Directed by Woody Allen
Written by Woody Allen, based on his play

Cast:
Ed Herlihy....	Narrator
Josef Sommer....	Ambassador Magee
Robert Stanton....	Mr. Burns
Edward Herrmann....	Mr. Kilroy
Rosemary Murphy....	Miss Pritchard
Michael J. Fox....	Axel Magee
Woody Allen....	Walter Hollander
Julie Kavner....	Marion Hollander
Mayim Bialik....	Susan Hollander
Austin Pendleton....	Chef Oscar
Dom DeLuise....	Father Drobney
Taina Elg....	Anna Gruber

Produced by Robert Greenhut
Executive Producers, J. E. Beaucaire, Jean Doumanian
Co-executive producer, Letty Aronson
Director of Photography, Carlo Di Palma
Film Editor, Susan E. Morse
Production Design, Santo Loquasto
Art Direction, Peter Eastman
Costume Design, Suzy Benzinger
Running time: 120 min

Mighty Aphrodite (1995)

Directed by Woody Allen
Written by Woody Allen

Cast:
F. Murray Abraham....	Greek Chorus Leader
Woody Allen....	Lenny
Helena Bonham Carter....	Amanda
J. Smith-Cameron....	Bud's Wife
Steven Randazzo....	Bud
David Ogden Stiers....	Laius
Olympia Dukakis....	Jocasta
Jeffrey Kurland....	Oedipus

Donald Symington....   Amanda's Father
Claire Bloom....   Amanda's Mother
Rosemary Murphy....   Adoption Coordinator
Paul Giamatti....   Extras Guild Researcher
Danielle Ferland....   Cassandra
Mira Sorvino....   Linda Ash
Jack Warden....   Tiresias

Produced by Robert Greenhut
Executive Producers, J. E. Beaucaire, Jean Doumanian
Co-executive Producers, Letty Aronson, Charles H. Joffe, Jack Rollins
Co-producer, Helen Robin
Associate Producer, Thomas Reilly
Original Music, Dick Hyman
Director of Photography, Carlo DiPalma
Film Editor, Susan E. Morse
Casting, Juliet Taylor
Production Design, Santo Loquasto
Art Direction, Tom Warren
Set Decoration, Susan Bode
Costume Design, Jeffrey Kurland
Production Manager, Helen Robin
Production Supervisor, Italy, Lucia Comelli
Production Manager, Italy, Paolo Pioggia
Production Manager, Italy, Michele Virgilio
Assistant Director, Thomas Reilly, Richard Patrick (second)
Running time: 98 min

Everyone Says I Love You (1996)

Directed by Woody Allen
Written by Woody Allen

Cast:
Edward Norton....   Holden Spence
Drew Barrymore....   Schuyler Dandridge
Alan Alda....   Bob Dandridge
Gaby Hoffmann....   Lane Dandridge
Natalie Portman....   Laura Dandridge
Lukas Haas....   Scott Dandridge
Goldie Hawn....   Steffi Dandridge
Itzhak Perlman....   Himself
Navah Perlman....   Pianist
Julia Roberts....   Von
Woody Allen....   Joe Berlin

Produced by Robert Greenhut
Executive Producers, J. E. Beaucaire, Jean Doumanian
Co-executive Producers, Letty Aronson, Charles H. Joffe, Jack Rollins
Co-producer, Helen Robin

Original Music, Dick Hyman
Songs:
    James Campbell Connelly, "If I Had You"
    Gus Kahn, "I'm Through with Love"
    Gus Kahn and Harry Ruby, "Makin' Whoopee"
    Bert Kalmar and Harry Ruby," Everyone Says I Love You," "Hooray for
        Captain Spaulding"
    Raymond Klages, "Just You, Just Me"
    Matty Malneck, "I'm Through with Love"
    Cole Porter, "Looking at You"
    Ted Shapiro, "If I Had You"
    Harry M. Woods, "What a Little Moonlight Can Do"

Director of Photography, Carlo Di Palma
Film Editor, Susan E. Morse
Casting, Juliet Taylor
Production Design, Santo Loquasto
Art Direction, Tom Warren
Set Decoration, Elaine O'Donnell
Costume Design, Jeffrey Kurland
Production Manager, Helen Robin
Assistant Director, Richard Patrick, Amy Lynn (second)
Special Effects, Connie Brink
Visual Effects, Randall Balsmeyer
Running time: 101 min

Deconstructing Harry (1997)

Directed by Woody Allen
Written by Woody Allen

Cast:

Caroline Aaron....	Doris
Woody Allen....	Harry Block
Kirstie Alley....	Joan
Bob Balaban....	Richard
Richard Benjamin....	Ken
Eric Bogosian....	Burt
Billy Crystal....	Larry
Judy Davis....	Lucy
Hazelle Goodman....	Cookie Williams
Mariel Hemingway....	Beth Kramer
Amy Irving....	Jane
Julie Kavner....	Grace
Eric Lloyd....	Hilly
Julia Louis-Dreyfus....	Leslie
Tobey Maguire....	Harvey Stern
Demi Moore....	Helen
Elizabeth Shue....	Fay

Stanley Tucci....	Paul Epstein
Robin Williams....	Mel
Philip Bosco....	Professor Clark
Gene Saks....	Harry's father
Stephanie Roth....	Janet

Produced by Jean Doumanian
Executive Producer, J. E. Beaucaire
Co-executive Producers, Letty Aronson, Charles H. Joffe, Jack Rollins
Co-producer, Richard Brick
Director of Photography, Carlo Di Palma
Film Editor, Susan E. Morse
Casting, Juliet Taylor
Production Design, Santo Loquasto
Art Direction, Tom Warren
Set Decoration, Susan Kaufman, Elaine O'Donnell
Costume Design, Suzy Benzinger
Production Manager, Charles Darby
Assistant Director, Richard Patrick, Lisa M. Rowe (second)
Special Effects Coordinator, John Ottesen
Running time: 96 min

Celebrity (1998)

Directed by Woody Allen
Written by Woody Allen

Cast:

Kenneth Branagh....	Lee Simon
Judy Davis....	Robin Simon
Joe Mantegna....	Tony Gardella
Famke Janssen....	Bonnie
Winona Ryder....	Nola
Charlize Theron....	Supermodel
Melanie Griffith....	Nicole Oliver
Michael Lerner....	Dr. Lupus
Leonardo DiCaprio....	Brandon Darrow
Hank Azaria....	David
Bebe Neuwirth...	Nina
Isaac Mizrahi....	Bruce Bishop
Gretchen Mol....	Vicky
Donald Trump....	Himself
Mary Jo Buttafuoco....	Herself
Joey Buttafuoco....	Himself
Jeffrey Wright....	Off Off Broadway Director
Kate Burton....	Cheryl, Robin's Friend
Greg Mottola....	Director
Dylan Baker....	Priest at Catholic Retreat
Andre Gregory....	John Papadakis

Patti D'Arbanville....	Iris
Allison Janney....	Evelyn Isaacs
Aida Turturro....	Psychic

Produced by Jean Doumanian
Executive Producer, J. E. Beaucaire
Co-executive Producers, Letty Aronson, Charles H. Joffe, Jack Rollins
Co-producer, Richard Brick
Director of Photography, Sven Nykvist
Film Editor, Susan E. Morse
Casting, Laura Rosenthal, Juliet Taylor
Production Design, Santo Loquasto
Art Direction, Tom Warren
Set Decoration, Susan Kaufman
Costume Design, Suzy Benzinger
Production Manager, Charles Darby
Assistant Directors, Richard Rosser, Richard Patrick,
    Marian G. Bostwick (second), Lisa M. Rowe (second),
    Peter Lauer (second unit director)
Special Effects Coordinator, Russell Berg
Visual Effects Producer, Camille Pirolo Geier
Visual effects Supervisor, Ellen Poon
Running time: 113 min

Sweet and Lowdown (1999)

Directed by Woody Allen
Written by Woody Allen

Cast:

Sean Penn....	Emmet Ray
Uma Thurman....	Blanche
Anthony LaPaglia....	Al Torrio
Samantha Morton....	Hattie
James Urbaniak....	Harry
Brian Markinson....	Bill Shields
John Waters....	Mr. Haynes
Gretchen Mol....	Ellie

Produced by Jean Doumanian
Executive Producer, J. E. Beaucaire
Co-executive Producers, Letty Aronson, Charles H. Joffe, Jack Rollins
Co-producer, Richard Brick
Original Music, Dick Hyman
Director of Photography, Zhao Fei
Film Editor, Alisa Lepselter
Casting, Laura Rosenthal, Juliet Taylor
Production Design, Santo Loquasto
Art Direction, Tom Warren
Set Decoration, Jessica Lanier
Costume Design, Laura Cunningham

Production Managers, Richard Brick, Margo Myers
Assistant Directors, Richard Patrick, Lisa Janowski, Brian A. York
Special Effects Coordinators, John Ottesen, Ron Ottesen
Running time: 95 min

Small-time Crooks (2000)

Directed by Woody Allen
Written by Woody Allen

Cast:

Woody Allen....	Ray Winkler
Tracey Ullman....	Frances 'Frenchy' Winkler
Hugh Grant....	David Grant
Elaine May....	May Sloan
Michael Rapaport....	Denny Doyle
Tony Darrow....	Tommy Beal
Jon Lovitz....	Benny Borkowshi
George Grizzard....	George Blint

Produced by Jean Doumanian
Executive Producer, J. E. Beaucaire
Co-executive Producers, Letty Aronson, Charles H. Joffe, Jack Rollins
Co-producer, Helen Robin
Director of Photography, Zhao Fei
Film Editor, Alisa Lepselter
Casting, Laura Rosenthal, Juliet Taylor
Production Design, Santo Loquasto
Art Direction, Tom Warren
Set Decoration, Jessica Lanier
Costume Design, Suzanne McCabe
Production Manager, Helen Robin
Assistant Director, Richard Patrick, Paul F. Bernard (second)
Running time: 94 min

The Curse of the Jade Scorpion (2001)

Directed by Woody Allen
Written by Woody Allen

Cast:

John Schuck....	Mize
Woody Allen....	C. W. Briggs
Helen Hunt....	Betty Ann Fitzgerald
Wallace Shawn....	George Bond
Dan Aykroyd....	Chris Magruder
Vince Giordano....	Rainbow Room All Star
David Ogden Stiers....	Voltan Polgar

Produced by Letty Aronson
Executive Producer, Stephen Tenenbaum

Co-executive Producers, Charles H. Joffe, Jack Rollins, Datty Ruth
Co-producer, Helen Robin
Director of Photography, Zhao Fei
Film Editor, Alisa Lepselter
Casting, Laura Rosenthal, Juliet Taylor
Production Design, Santo Loquasto
Art Direction, Tom Warren
Set Decoration, Jessica Lanier
Costume Design, Suzanne McCabe
Production Manager, Helen Robin
Production Supervisor, Janice Williams
Assistant Director, Sam Hoffman, Joan G. Bostwick (second)
Special Effects Coordinators, John Ottesen, Ron Ottesen
Running time: 103 min

Hollywood Ending (2002)

Directed by Woody Allen
Written by Woody Allen

Cast:

Woody Allen....	Val Waxman
Téa Leoni....	Ellie
George Hamilton....	Ed
Debra Messing....	Lori Fox
Mark Rydell....	Al Hack
Treat Williams....	Hal Jaeger
Isaac Mizrahi....	Elio Sebastian
Marian Seldes....	Alexandra
Aaron Stanford....	Actor
Tiffani Thiessen....	Sharon Bates
Yu Lu....	Cameraman
Barney Cheng....	Translator

Produced by Letty Aronson
Executive Producer, Stephen Tenenbaum
Co-executive Producers, Charles H. Joffe, Jack Rollins
Co-producer, Helen Robin
Director of Photography, Wedigo von Schultzendorff
Film Editor, Alisa Lepselter
Casting, Laura Rosenthal, Juliet Taylor
Production Design, Santo Loquasto
Art Direction, Tom Warren
Set Decoration, Regina Graves
Costume Design, Melissa Toth
Production Manager, Helen Robin
Production Supervisor, Janice Williams
Assistant Director, Richard Patrick, Danielle Rigby (second)
Running time: 114 min

Index

gangsters, fondness for, 152, 153, 154; Hope, Bob, influence of, 80, 81, 82, 83; independence of, 6; influences of, 100, 101; Jewish aspects of, 38, 39, 40; and magic realism, 8, 17, 18, 19, 27–28, 29, 31, 32, 42, 46, 47, 49, 50, 55, 140–142, 143, 144, 145; marketing of, 177, 178; mass media, uneasiness toward, 68; milieu of, 7; movies, love of, 74, 75, 76, 78; name change of, 89; New York, love of, 20, 35, 36, 37, 83, 84, 85, 88; as performer, 6, 114; and personal life, 6; philosophy of, 138; physical humor of, 23; as playwright, 6, 73, 76; popularity, in Europe, 16, 178; Previn, Soon-Yi, relationship with, 65; private life, 61, 65; productivity of, 25, 26; relationships, as theme, 111, 133, 137, 140; scandal, 61, 62, 63, 65; screen persona of, 13, 82, 124, 125, 127, 168; self-evaluation of, 25, 26, 121, 123, 162, 163; staff writer, at NBC, 91; as stand-up comic, 13, 39; as storyteller, 74; style of, 7, 50, 51, 56, 109, 164; and tabloid press, 63, 64, 65; themes of, 8, 10, 41, 52, 58, 63, 68, 69, 110, 111, 114, 133, 137, 140, 156, 157, 175; uncertainty, as theme, 157, 158; vision of, 68; as workaholic, myth of, 146, 147; as writer, 5, 73, 92
Anastasia, Albert, 153

Anhedonia, 108
Annie Hall (character), 19, 113, 114
Annie Hall (film), 7, 13, 15, 34, 38, 41, 93, 94, 107, 127, 177; as Academy Award winner, 14, 113, 114; commercial success of, 14; magic realism in, 19, 145; origins of, 108; popularity of, 113; as turning point, 109, 110; themes of, 111, 112, 114
Another Woman, 15, 23, 41, 46; themes of, 147, 148
Ash, Linda, 55
Astaire, Fred, 77, 139

Bananas, 8, 11, 82, 95, 101, 121; absurdity of, 21; Chaplin, Charles, imitation of, 102, 103; structure of, 93, 94
Bankhead, Tallulah, 54
Bates, Sandy, 11, 12, 13, 27, 34
Baxter, Tom, 30
Bellow, Saul, 29
Bergman, Ingmar, 6, 23, 66, 69, 109, 137, 157
Bicycle Thief, The, 119
Bjorkman, Stig, 52
Bloch, Harry, 55
Bogart, Humphrey, 78
Bogdanovich, Peter, 101
Boxer, Sarah, 24
Branagh, Kenneth, 57, 58, 59, 132, 133
Brando, Marlon, 100
Brickman, Marshall, 19, 20, 108, 112, 126, 166
Broadbent, Jim, 54